Development Co-operation
Review Series

CANADA

1998 No. 26

Development Assistance Committee

ORGANISATION FOR ECONOMIC CO-OPERATION AND DEVELOPMENT

ORGANISATION FOR ECONOMIC CO-OPERATION AND DEVELOPMENT

Pursuant to Article 1 of the Convention signed in Paris on 14th December 1960, and which came into force on 30th September 1961, the Organisation for Economic Co-operation and Development (OECD) shall promote policies designed:

- to achieve the highest sustainable economic growth and employment and a rising standard of living in Member countries, while maintaining financial stability, and thus to contribute to the development of the world economy;
- to contribute to sound economic expansion in Member as well as non-member countries in the process of economic development; and
- to contribute to the expansion of world trade on a multilateral, non-discriminatory basis in accordance with international obligations.

The original Member countries of the OECD are Austria, Belgium, Canada, Denmark, France, Germany, Greece, Iceland, Ireland, Italy, Luxembourg, the Netherlands, Norway, Portugal, Spain, Sweden, Switzerland, Turkey, the United Kingdom and the United States. The following countries became Members subsequently through accession at the dates indicated hereafter: Japan (28th April 1964), Finland (28th January 1969), Australia (7th June 1971), New Zealand (29th May 1973), Mexico (18th May 1994), the Czech Republic (21st December 1995), Hungary (7th May 1996), Poland (22nd November 1996) and Korea (12th December 1996). The Commission of the European Communities takes part in the work of the OECD (Article 13 of the OECD Convention).

In order to achieve its aims the OECD has set up a number of specialised committees. One of these is the Development Assistance Committee, whose Members have agreed to secure an expansion of aggregate volume of resources made available to developing countries and to improve their effectiveness. To this end, Members periodically review together both the amount and the nature of their contributions to aid programmes, bilateral and multilateral, and consult each other on all other relevant aspects of their development assistance policies.

The Members of the Development Assistance Committee are Australia, Austria, Belgium, Canada, Denmark, Finland, France, Germany, Ireland, Italy, Japan, Luxembourg, the Netherlands, New Zealand, Norway, Portugal, Spain, Sweden, Switzerland, the United Kingdom, the United States and the Commission of the European Communities.

Publié en français sous le titre :
SÉRIE DES EXAMENS EN MATIÈRE DE COOPÉRATION POUR LE DÉVELOPPEMENT
CANADA

FOREWORD

The Development Assistance Committee (DAC) conducts periodic reviews to improve the individual and collective development co-operation efforts of DAC Members. The policies and efforts of individual Members are critically examined approximately once every three years. Some six programmes are examined annually.

The Peer Review is prepared by a team, consisting of representatives of the Secretariat working with officials from two DAC Members who are designated as examiners. The Member under review provides a memorandum setting out the main developments in its policies and programmes. Then the Secretariat and the examiners visit the capital to interview officials, parliamentarians, and NGO representatives of the donor to obtain a first-hand insight into current issues surrounding the development co-operation efforts of the Member concerned. Brief field visits investigate how Members have absorbed the major DAC policies, principles and concerns, and examine operations in recipient countries, particularly with regard to sustainability, gender equality and other aspects of participatory development, and local aid co-ordination.

Putting all this information and analysis together, the Secretariat prepares a draft report on the Member's development co-operation which is the basis for the DAC review meeting. At this meeting senior officials from the Member under review discuss a series of questions posed in a brief document: 'Main issues for the Review'. These questions are formulated by the Secretariat in association with the examiners. The main discussion points and operational policy recommendations emerging from the review meeting are set out in the Summary and Conclusions section of the publication.

This publication contains the Summary and Conclusions as agreed by the Committee following its review on 22 January 1998 in Paris, and the Report prepared by the Secretariat in association with the examiners, representing the Netherlands and New Zealand, on the development co-operation policies and efforts of Canada. The report is published on the authority of the Secretary-General of the OECD.

James Michel
DAC Chair

LIST OF ACRONYMS

ANC	African National Congress
APEC	Asia-Pacific Economic Co-operation
APMs	Anti-personnel mines
CCICED	China Council for International Co-operation on Environment and Development
CEECs	Central and Eastern European Countries
CIDA	Canadian International Development Agency
DAC	Development Assistance Committee
DFAIT	Department of Foreign Affairs and International Trade
EIA	Environmental impact assessment
GEF	Global Environment Facility
GDP	Gross domestic product
GNP	Gross national product
HIPC	Heavily-indebted poor countries
ICHRDD	International Centre for Human Rights and Democratic Development
ICRC	International Commission of the Red Cross
IDASA	Institute for Democracy in South Africa
IDRC	International Development Research Centre
IFIs	International financial institutions
IHA	International Humanitarian Assistance
IISD	International Institute for Sustainable Development
IMF	International Monetary Fund
INC	Industrial Co-operation
LRC	Legal Resource Centre

NAFTA	North American Free-Trade Agreement
NEPA	National Environmental Protection Agency
NGOs	Non-governmental organisations
NIS	New Independent States of the former Soviet Union
OA	Official aid
ODA	Official development assistance
SAGA	Structural Adjustment and Gender in Africa
UN	United Nations
UNDP	United Nations Development Programme
UNICEF	United Nations Children's Fund
WID	Women in development
WHO	World Health Organisation
WTO	World Trade Organisation

Exchange rates (C$ per US$) were:

1994	1995	1996
1.3659	1.3728	1.3638

Signs used

()	Secretariat estimate in whole or part
–	Nil
0.0	Negligible
..	Not available
...	Not available separately but included in total
n.a.	Not applicable

Slight discrepancies in totals are due to rounding

TABLE OF CONTENTS

Part II
BASIC PROFILES

Tables

Figures

Charts

Boxes

SUMMARY AND CONCLUSIONS

OVERVIEW

In the context of rapidly-changing domestic and international challenges looking towards the new century, the Canadian government's foreign policy statement – *Canada in the World* – set out a comprehensive agenda for Canada's foreign policy and development co-operation. Based on a major national consultation effort, the statement renewed and updated Canada's commitment to an active role in collective approaches to the creation of a better world. The high ambitions that Canada has set for itself continue a long tradition of constructive engagement in world affairs and development efforts, a tradition that both draws upon and nourishes Canada's national identity. A recent historic manifestation of this tradition is Canada's contribution to concluding the treaty to ban antipersonnel landmines, signed in Ottawa in December 1997. Another recent initiative was the Global Knowledge Conference, held in Toronto in June 1997, co-sponsored by the Canadian International Development Agency (CIDA) with the World Bank, the United Nations Development Programme and others, with the aim of highlighting the new challenges and opportunities for developing countries in an age where the knowledge/communications revolution is a powerful new factor in development. These two initiatives illustrate Canada's special ability to help lead the international community towards action which pushes out the frontiers of international co-operation.

The prominent international role that Canada has set for itself has not, however, been accompanied by increases in resources allocated for development co-operation. On the contrary, in the context of a fundamental fiscal adjustment to respond to its domestic public debt burden, Canada's official development assistance (ODA) effort has declined significantly, from an average of approximately 0.45 per cent of gross national product (GNP) at the beginning of the 1990s to 0.32 per cent in 1996 (see Figure 1). The ODA/GNP ratio is projected to fall still further by 1998/99, to below 0.30 per cent.

At the same time, the ministries and agencies charged with the prosecution of Canada's foreign policy and development agenda have taken important reform measures to equip themselves with the necessary human resources and institutional systems and structures to tackle the expanded missions set for them in *Canada in the World* in a coherent and co-ordinated fashion. But they face an increasing mismatch between the scope of their mandate and the diminishing means at their disposal. Reductions in ODA, combined with a growing range of goals, brings into sharper focus, for example, the issue of the wide dispersion of Canadian aid efforts. It is already clear that ODA budget cuts have reduced programming in many partner countries to levels at which past activities can no longer be continued and previous leadership roles have to be relinquished.

Canada has exercised important influence at the multilateral level, based on the quality of its analyses, the effort invested in multilateral governing bodies, and also derived in the past from Canada's readiness to provide a relatively high share of the financing of a number of multilateral organisations and regional development banks. This positive influence stands to suffer now that Canada is no longer prepared to make its traditional extra effort in financing multilateral development co-operation.

Thus, at the end of the 1990s, there is a paradox at the heart of Canada's internationalism. The determination continues to be involved in a very wide range of issues and with as wide a range of partners and multilateral organisations as possible, while the aid budget has been cut by 29 per cent over six years. This paradox raises concerns about Canada's ability to meet expectations about Canada's role in the world, both at home and internationally.

Figure 1. **ODA net disbursements**
At constant 1995 prices and as a share of GNP

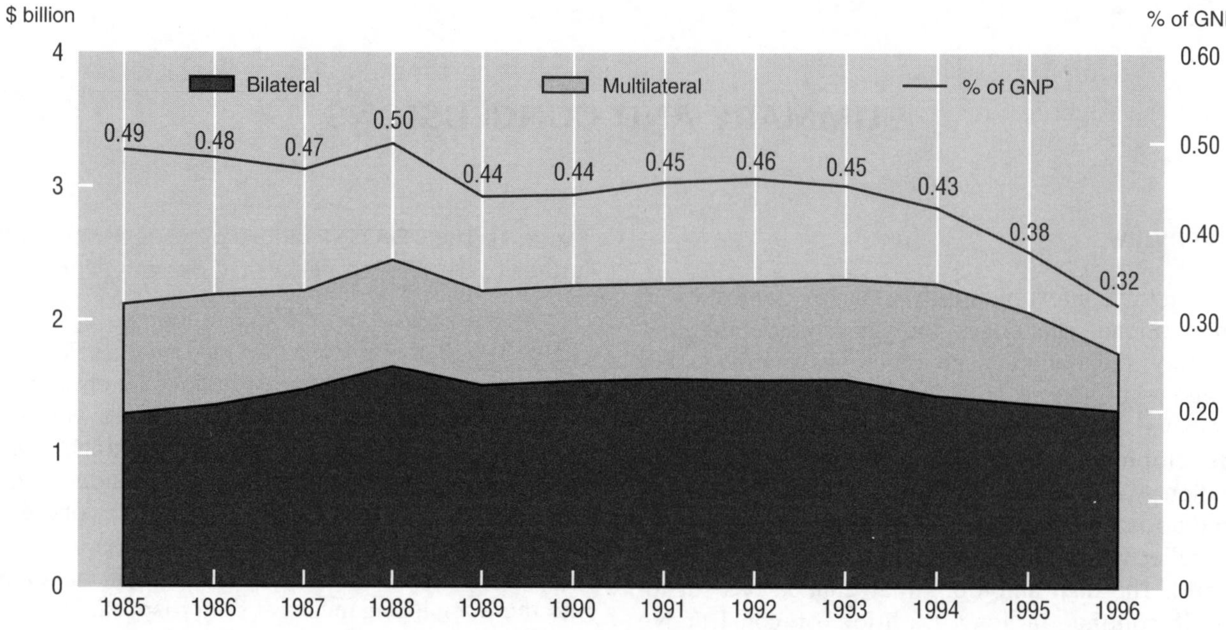

Source : OECD.

CANADA IN THE WORLD: A NEW VISION OF CANADA'S INTERNATIONAL ROLE

Canada in the World outlines a new vision for the role of Canadian foreign policy based on three objectives:

- the promotion of prosperity and employment;
- the protection of Canada's security within a stable global framework; and
- the projection of Canadian values and culture.

Canada in the World points to development co-operation as "an important instrument in support of these objectives, and indeed as an investment in prosperity and employment".

Canada in the World also places special emphasis on the need for coherent responses to global challenges and specifically mandates the different Canadian actors involved to co-ordinate their efforts. Various inter-ministerial co-ordination mechanisms have been established to this effect. In particular, the Department of Foreign Affairs and International Trade's (DFAIT's) recently created Global and Human Issues Bureau is charged with ensuring coherent responses to international issues ranging from the global environment, to child labour, to international crime and preventive diplomacy.

Canada's foreign policy is also characterised by intense efforts to identify and analyse forthcoming global shifts and challenges, with a view to formulating effective and timely responses. "Canada 2005", a government-wide policy research effort to identify critical issues for Canada including competitiveness, economic integration and human security, is an illustration of the intellectual investment being made.

With the current Ministers for Foreign Affairs, International Trade, and Finance all having experience and interest in development matters, together with the Cabinet-ranked Minister for International Co-operation, there is a strong team at Cabinet level. Meetings of Cabinet thus function as the ultimate policy co-ordination forum for Canada's programme. However, with three ministers successively holding the International Co-operation portfolio since January 1996, the continuity of strong and sustained promotion of the core development co-operation programme at the political level has suffered.

At the same time, alongside the longer-term goals for development co-operation, *Canada in the World* also promotes the objective of enhancing trade with developing countries with attendant benefits to employment in Canada. A series of high-profile trade promotion missions, led by the Prime Minister ("Team Canada") have focused on fast-growing developing countries. This focus, in combination with the aid budget cuts, has led some in Canada to see a shift in priorities in relations with developing countries, driven by budgetary and commercial concerns. Meanwhile, Canada's politically visible initiatives on international issues such as child labour and landmines have served to focus the attention of the Canadian public on particular sets of development issues, while the overall resources allocated to development co-operation have declined.

THE CANADIAN INTERNATIONAL DEVELOPMENT AGENCY (CIDA): AN AGENCY IN RENEWAL

Canada in the World pointed to the need for a redirection of Canada's development co-operation activities in order to meet new challenges, and a clearer definition of objectives and stricter evaluation of the actual impacts of ODA-supported programmes. Over the past few years, CIDA has embarked on a comprehensive and thorough renewal process, aimed at addressing the twin objectives of operationalising the mandate provided by *Canada in the World* and improving programme delivery practices.

Efforts to improve the focus and contents of programmes have concentrated on the formulation of a range of policy guidelines to translate the directions given in *Canada in the World* into concrete programmes. CIDA's *Policy on Poverty Reduction*, adopted in June 1995, provides an overarching analytical link among the set of priorities with which CIDA works: basic human needs; gender equity; infrastructure services; human rights, democracy and good governance; private sector development; and environment. These themes and priorities match well with the common strategy document adopted by Development Assistant Committee (DAC) Members in May 1996, *Shaping the 21st Century: The Contribution of Development Co-operation*, which CIDA has adopted as a central reference point in its own corporate goals.

Taken together, CIDA's programme priorities represent a formidable agenda for any agency to take on. It is not the intention for each of CIDA's country and other programmes to address all these challenges simultaneously. While environment and gender equality are treated by CIDA as fundamental cross-cutting concerns that are addressed in all activities, the objective for CIDA's geographical branches is to formulate coherent programmes consistent with one or more priorities in line with the needs and circumstances of partner countries and to complement activities of other donors. The definition of measurable and realistic objectives, consistent with available financial and human resources, is another key challenge.

The Agency has made major progress towards redirecting its bilateral programmes from a traditional sector-focus to a theme-based approach, with a clear concentration on results, rather than inputs. The relationship between some of these themes would however merit further clarification. The distinction between the poverty reduction and the basic human needs objectives, for example, seems not always to be fully understood by staff, so that the translation of the poverty reduction thrust into country programmes still has some way to go. (Encouragingly, the new CIDA programme framework for Tanzania, issued in September 1997, shows how this can be done.) Much work also remains on the classification and statistical reporting of activities in line with these themes, as required by *Canada in the World*.

CIDA has made major strides in building the human rights and governance dimension into its programme priorities and design in all aspects of its operations. This work includes a good deal of low-key, but strategically critical, support for organisations in developing countries promoting and defending civil rights, constitutional government and democratic processes. This coherent, broad approach reflects a high level of integration between a variety of development co-operation policies, such as humanitarian assistance in emergency situations and longer-term development co-operation aiming at poverty reduction, equity and sustainable economic growth. CIDA is also active in the area of conflict prevention and peacebuilding and, together with DFAIT, has created a new Canadian structure for organising rapid responses to emergency situations with volunteer and non-governmental organisation assistance.

a) Results-based management and a learning organisation

Efforts towards improving the effectiveness of its programme delivery systems have been similarly thorough, spurred by internal assessments pointing in similar directions to the findings of a 1993 Report by the Auditor-General of Canada which highlighted a need for improvement in programme management practices. The exemplary relationship that has subsequently developed between the Auditor-General and CIDA, aiming at identifying and addressing critical areas of weakness and monitoring progress, is noteworthy. This relationship is succeeding in transforming the management culture in CIDA, changing the "mindset" of staff to focus much more on results and impacts of programmes and projects, and injecting fresh energy and morale into the Agency. These changes have been accompanied by a comprehensive initiative to renew CIDA staff, both in terms of age and skills composition, and a large investment in training. In the process, CIDA has moved to the front ranks of the Canadian public sector in terms of its human resource management and the creation of a results-based management culture.

With the introduction of results-based management and the emphasis placed on continuous assessment and monitoring of projects, a "portfolio management" approach has quickly emerged in the geographical branches. This allows a clearer view of the "state of play" across the whole range of projects and programmes, and permits more timely and effective linking between programme managers at all levels, and, most importantly, between Ottawa and the field. Thus the whole management system is being streamlined and speeded up, with early identification of problems and opportunities and the implementation of corrective measures long before programme completion.

Another important management reform is the dissolution of CIDA's professional branch, with its personnel now distributed among the geographical units, although a core has been allocated to the Policy Branch, giving it a multidisciplinary capacity and strengthening its ability to affect the programming process. As in a number of other aid agencies which have also taken this step, including the World Bank and the Department for International Development in the United Kingdom, the various categories of professionals are being linked across the Agency through "networks" which share experience and new knowledge. There is also a strong network devoted to promoting best practices for local capacity development, an issue which CIDA actively advances on the international level.

In sum, CIDA's efforts to become a "learning organisation" have taken a leap forward. More broadly, the reform process has made CIDA a much more integrated and policy and performance driven organisation than it was at the time of the last DAC Review of Canada in June 1994. A major programme is underway to devise and introduce a new unified management information system to support the new management approach.

At the same time, the practice of results-based management highlights the dilemmas faced by many donors in their attempt to develop genuine partnerships with recipients. The essential challenge is to reconcile the needs, objectives and leadership responsibilities of developing-country partners with the demanding accountability criteria required of CIDA by the government, the Parliament and the Canadian public.

b) Managing diverse partnerships

There is a larger issue here as well for Canada, a country which has made a special point of building its development co-operation around the concept and practice of Canadian partnerships. Canadian aid at its best sees a strong fusion of Canadian partnerships with the development partnership on the ground, with some outstanding examples, such as the co-operation with South Africa described later in this Report. The International Development Research Centre (IDRC) carries this principle through to the international level, as a notable expression of Canada's partnership philosophy. The *Canada in the World* statement reinforces this orientation towards enlisting Canadian organisations and interests in its development co-operation efforts, while recognising that public support for aid in Canada (as in other DAC countries) is overwhelmingly based on altruistic and humanitarian motives.

The challenge is to ensure that Canadian initiative, partnerships and accountability systems reinforce rather than weaken the all-important partnerships with developing countries, and that the process of managing Canadian stakeholders and their multiple objectives does not impair development objectives. There is potential tension between the impulses for partnerships in the field and in Canada. Canadian institutions and solutions are often highly appropriate and valued by developing country partners but this may not always be the case, or adaptation to local needs may be inadequate.

Canada's extensive use of tied aid is an area where this tension can be most acute. As part of the Canadian government's overall concern with accountability and the impact of public expenditures, there would seem to be a strong case for Canada, like other donors, to re-examine the efficiency of tied aid as a means of promoting exports and employment, alongside the costs and benefits of tied aid for developing countries receiving Canadian ODA.

A further source of tension in Canadian aid management is the balance between centralised and decentralised management of country programmes. After a major (and, in some respects, excessive) decentralisation effort began to prove costly and difficult to manage, CIDA has now "recentralised" with its country directors and programme managers located in Ottawa. The largest field offices have five or six CIDA professionals, but most have only two and some just one. However, in countries with a substantial country programme these field offices are usually supported by significant Project Support Units, including local professional and administrative staff. It remains to be seen whether the slim CIDA presence in the field is fully compatible with the demands for improved field-based partnerships and donor co-ordination in developing countries, notably in increasingly complex areas such as poverty reduction and governance. Moreover, the limitations of centralisation might become more apparent in the event that the Canadian programme were restored as a greater critical mass in partner countries.

CANADA'S ODA VOLUME: A CRITICAL TURNING POINT FOR CANADA

The previous Review of Canada by the Development Assistance Committee had raised the concern that insufficient resources could undermine Canada's ability to pursue its ambitious policy objectives. This concern is even more pressing today.

Final revised expenditure figures are not available at the time of writing to support a precise comparison with other areas of Canadian federal expenditure. However, it is clear that the International Assistance Envelope has been one of the most heavily cut items in the federal government budget. With the further cuts already programmed, the projected reduction in the Envelope between 1993-94 and 1998-99 is C$ 767 million or around 29 per cent, more than twice the reduction level of the federal budget as a whole. A substantial and sustained effort will be required in the future if Canada's ODA/GNP ratio is to return to its level of the beginning of the 1990s, *i.e.* around 0.45 per cent. Even a lesser growth objective, which would still imply a retreat from Canada's previous aid volume targets, would present a major challenge for political decision-making on budget priorities. (See Figure 2 in Chapter 1.)

In early 1998, the Minister for Finance will present a new federal budget to Parliament. While the previously-announced cuts in the International Assistance Envelope for 1998-99 are expected to be confirmed at that time, an announcement of a further decline in the International Assistance Envelope for 1999-2000 would be a fundamental setback to prospects for a recovery in Canada's ODA volume. Even holding the aid budget constant would involve a further decline in ODA/GNP performance. An increase of around 5 per cent would be needed simply for Canada's ODA not to lose any further ground in relation to current GNP growth. Even if Canada's ODA were to increase by one percentage point faster than GNP each year, it would take half a century for Canada to regain the 0.45 per cent of GNP level. The budget choices will be critical for the future impact of Canada's ODA programme, and Canada's valued international role.

Part I

KEY TRENDS IN POLICIES AND ORGANISATION

STRATEGIC DIRECTIONS AND FINANCIAL COMMITMENTS

A. CANADA'S 1995 FOREIGN POLICY STATEMENT: *CANADA IN THE WORLD*

Few donors have questioned, re-oriented and revitalised their development co-operation programme as often as Canada. These processes of reflection and renewal have underpinned Canada's active and innovative contribution to international development. Canada's foreign policy, including international economic and trade relations, is now based on the February 1995 government statement *Canada in the World*. As regards official development assistance (ODA), this statement replaces the 1988 strategy *Sharing our Future*.

Canada in the World was the culmination of a comprehensive process of consultations and deliberations to review Canada's foreign policy to ensure that it reflected changing domestic and international realities. The statement describes the evolving context for foreign policy, Canada's objectives within that evolving context and how the government intends to pursue those objectives.

The review found that Canadians want to remain actively involved in the world, although they recognise the financial constraints Canada faces. Consistent with these findings, *Canada in the World* identifies three interdependent and mutually-reinforcing objectives for Canadian foreign policy:

- the promotion of prosperity and employment;
- the protection of Canada's security, within a stable global framework; and
- the projection of Canadian values (respect for human rights, democracy, the rule of law and the environment) and culture.

Canada in the World identifies international assistance as a key instrument, complementing diplomacy and trade in the pursuit of these objectives:

"[International assistance] is an investment in **prosperity and employment**. It connects the Canadian economy to some of the world's fastest-growing markets – the markets of the devel-oping world. And, in the long-run, development co-operation can help lift developing countries out of poverty. This means that it contributes to a stronger global economy in which Canadians, and other peoples, can grow and prosper. International assistance also contributes to **global security** by tackling many key threats to human security such as the abuse of human rights, disease, environmental degradation, population growth and the widening gap between rich and poor. Finally, it is one of the clearest international expressions of **Canadian values and culture** – of Canadians' desire to help the less fortunate and of their strong sense of social justice – and an effective means of sharing these values with the rest of the world."

[*Canada in the World*, page 40, original emphasis]

The statement reaffirms the Canadian government's commitment to making progress towards the ODA target of 0.7 per cent of gross national product (GNP) when Canada's fiscal situation allows it. While committing Canada to providing most of its ODA to low-income countries and to devoting the highest share of resources to African countries, *Canada in the World* highlights the growing importance for Canada of relations with countries in Latin America, the Caribbean and the Asia-Pacific region.

Canada in the World places great emphasis on the need for co-ordination and coherence between the different instruments of foreign policy and established the Foreign Affairs Policy Co-ordination Committee to "oversee systematic policy co-ordination between the Department of Foreign Affairs and International Trade and the Canadian International Development Agency". Following the appointment of a separate Minister for International Co-operation in January 1996, this Committee was replaced by as-needed meetings of Ministers and Secretaries of State. The Ministers for Foreign Affairs, International Trade, Finance and International Co-operation are all cabinet-level appointments and so Cabinet is now the highest forum for policy debate and shared decision making as regards development co-operation.

In response to another directive in *Canada in the World*, the Global and Human Issues Bureau was created within the Department of Foreign Affairs and Trade (DFAIT) in 1995 "to help bring greater coherence to the government's capacity to address internationally such issues as the global environment, population growth, international migration (including refugee issues), international crime, human rights, democratisation, preventive diplomacy and post-conflict peacebuilding". The creation of this Bureau strengthens DFAIT's leadership role, as described in the foreign policy statement, in ensuring "the greatest possible coherence and synergy over the full range of the Government's international activities in order to ensure that [Canada is] effective in pursuing [its] key objectives". The Bureau works collaboratively with other government departments, including the Canadian International Development Agency (CIDA), to ensure that their views are properly reflected in Canadian foreign policy positions concerning global issues.

Canada in the World emphasizes the essential complementarity between efforts conducted at the bilateral and multilateral levels and confirms Canada's long-standing emphasis on multilateral approaches to global issues. The multilateral system is seen as a critical vehicle for exercising influence in global affairs, beyond Canada's relative economic or political weight, based on the strength of policy and intellectual contributions. Canada's positions in international development institutions, conferences and summits are the subject of inter-departmental discussions involving all departments concerned.

In line with the forward-looking and multidisciplinary approaches to global issues embodied in *Canada in the World*, the Canadian government is active in exploring broader co-ordination and coherence issues relating to the links between domestic policy making, globalisation and international policies. The government-wide *Canada 2005 Policy Research* exercise, launched by the Clerk of the Privy Council Office in 1996, has served to identify critical pressure points on Canadian society to 2005 and establish an appropriate government research agenda. This exercise has a broad international perspective and addresses key concerns such as competitiveness, economic integration and human security. It aims to foster a greater understanding of international issues among more domestic-oriented departments. It has resulted in an exchange of views, opinions and experiences and is helping to promote a stronger willingness to work together and to take a broader perspective on some important issues.

Canada's foreign policy framework clearly reflects a careful analysis of current and future global challenges. A high degree of inter-departmental co-ordination with regard to policy formulation in the areas of trade, development and other important areas of foreign policy is evident. At the same time, *Canada in the World* conveys mixed messages as regards the relative priority of Canada's trade, development and other foreign policy objectives. High-profile trade missions in recent years to a number of developing countries have created the impression that Canada's foreign policy agenda is largely driven by trade objectives.

This impression is however counter-balanced by Canada's leadership in addressing a number of pressing issues on the international agenda, ranging from landmines to peacebuilding, to exploitative child labour, to United Nations (UN) reform. These initiatives are discussed further in Chapter 2.

B. CANADA'S DEVELOPMENT CO-OPERATION: PRIORITIES AND MANAGEMENT DIRECTIVES

Canada in the World sets out a clear mandate for Canadian ODA, centred on poverty reduction:

> "The purpose of Canada's ODA is to support sustainable development in developing countries, in order to reduce poverty and to contribute to a more secure, equitable and prosperous world."

[*Canada in the World*, page 42]

Canada recognises that there cannot be a single approach to poverty reduction. Efforts to help the poor must rely on an array of programmes and policies, at various levels and tailored to the specific circumstances of the partner country. The foreign policy statement consequently mandates Canadian ODA to concentrate available resources on six programme priorities: basic human needs; women in development (WID); infrastructure services; human rights, democracy and good governance; private sector development; and environment.

Canada played an influential role during reflections in the Development Assistance Committee (DAC) which resulted in the adoption of *Shaping the 21st Century: The Contribution of Development*

Co-operation. The *Shaping the 21st Century* strategy gave further impetus to the mandate and programme priorities for Canadian ODA embodied in *Canada in the World*. Given the close match between the two visions, Canada is relatively advanced in its efforts to implement the *Shaping the 21st Century* strategy. Recently elaborated policies relating to basic human needs, health and children specifically address pertinent *Shaping the 21st Century* goals.

In addition to setting forth a clear mandate and priorities, *Canada in the World* sets out three other key commitments for Canadian ODA: strengthened development partnerships, improved effectiveness and better reporting of results.

Strengthened development partnerships

Canada in the World emphasizes the importance of responding to the needs and priorities of the partner country and the need to encourage local participation and ownership, based on an in-depth knowledge of local conditions. This commitment clearly mirrors the partnership principle at the centre of the *Shaping the 21st Century* strategy. CIDA increasingly operates by supporting partnerships between Canadian organisations and developing country organisations. In practice, these links are originated mainly by Canadian civil society and private sector. The tying of aid to procurement is seen in this perspective by Canada as a mechanism for increasing partnerships between the ODA programme and Canadian businesses, and for encouraging the involvement of Canadian voluntary- and private-sector actors in international development issues.

Improved effectiveness

Improved effectiveness includes efforts to streamline and improve the effectiveness and efficiency of Canada's ODA activities, focusing on the quality and sustainability of results rather than on inputs. Important steps have has been taken in this direction, which are addressed in Chapter 3.

Better reporting of results

Canadian ODA is committed to paying special attention to establishing clear objectives for programmes and projects and to reporting their results to Parliament and the public. This includes the government sharing more widely the results of evaluations and lessons learnt to better inform the public,

as well as Canadian, multilateral and bilateral partners. This commitment to report results better is in line with efforts by other DAC Members to monitor efforts to achieve the quantitative and qualitative goals of the *Shaping the 21st Century* strategy. A report on the results of CIDA's activities is now prepared annually and presented to Parliament. Since 1996, results are reported for each of the six ODA programme priorities with specific information provided on the benefits for Canada.

C. THE BUDGET PROCESS AND FUTURE PROSPECTS FOR CANADIAN ODA

Canada's development co-operation programme is mostly funded by the federal government's International Assistance Envelope. Some 95 per cent of activities funded by the Envelope qualify for recording as ODA, the remainder is official aid (OA). In addition to activities funded through this Envelope, other costs and expenditures qualify for recording as ODA, such as the costs of maintaining refugees and debt relief.

Final revised expenditure figures are not available at the time of writing to allow a precise comparison with other areas of Canadian federal expenditure. However, it is clear that the International Assistance Envelope has been one of the most heavily cut items in the federal government budget. With the further cuts already programmed, the projected reduction in the Envelope between 1993-94 and 1998-99 is C$ 767 million or around 29 per cent, more than twice the reduction level of the federal budget as a whole.

Against a background of sustained GNP growth, projected cuts to the International Assistance Envelope imply that Canada's ODA/GNP ratio will continue to fall in future. On the basis of net ODA figures calculated by the North-South Institute[1] and GNP estimates prepared by the Conference Board of Canada,[2] ODA commitments as a share of GNP will fall from 0.35 per cent in the 1996-97 fiscal year to 0.29 per cent in 1997-98 and 0.26 per cent in 1998-99, as compared to an average ratio of around 0.45 per cent in the early 1990s.

The Secretariat has prepared an extrapolation[3] which illustrates the effort Canada would subsequently need to make for its ODA/GNP ratio to return to its level of the beginning of the 1990s, *i.e.* 0.45 per cent (see Figure 2). The International Assistance Envelope would need to increase each year in line with GNP growth if the ODA/GNP ratio is

Figure 2. **Future prospects for Canadian ODA**

ODA commitments as a share of GNP

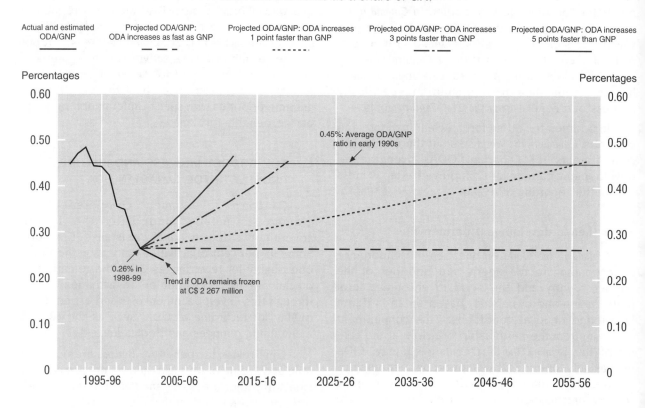

1. The North-South Institute estimates ODA in 1998-99 of C$ 2 267 million.
2. GNP forecasts 1996-97 to 1998-99: Conference Board of Canada.
Source: OECD.

not to fall any further. Even if ODA were to increase by one percentage point faster than GNP each year, it would take half a century to regain the 0.45 per cent level. If ODA were to increase annually by five percentage points faster than GNP, it would take more than a decade to attain a level of 0.45 per cent.

Cuts to the International Assistance Envelope and other federal programmes need to be seen in the broader context of the Canadian political and economic situation in the 1990s. When the Liberal government took office after the October 1993 elections, it inherited a federal budget deficit of C$ 42 billion, the equivalent of 5.9 per cent of gross domestic product (GDP). The new government made deficit reduction one of its main objectives and started a programme of cuts affecting most government activities. The government also reduced from five to two years the horizon for rolling fiscal targets, meaning that difficult budget decisions had

to be addressed within a shorter time frame. The Minister for Finance's annual budget speech to Parliament now covers two fiscal years. It modifies or confirms the previously-announced projected budget for the up-coming fiscal year and gives an indication for the subsequent fiscal year.

Policies to bring down Canada's budget deficit have been effective. Aided by an expanding economy and lower interest payments on its public debt, Canada has reduced its deficit more quickly than expected. In October 1997, the Minister for Finance was able to announce that the deficit for 1996-97 had been C$ 8.9 billion (1.1 per cent of GDP) and that a balanced budget would be attained by 1998-99, at the latest. In its recent economic survey of Canada, the OECD's Economic and Development Review Committee noted that fiscal consolidation has been largely achieved through a process of downsizing and restructuring that has involved a great deal of hardship in Canada, contributing to job insecurity and low consumer confidence. In such a context, it is not surprising that after all these sacrifices pressures have been mounting within the country for a "fiscal dividend", in the form of tax cuts and higher government spending. Given the relatively high level of public debt – at around 70 per cent, the net debt-to-GDP ratio remains the third highest among OECD countries for which comparable data are available – priority should be given to putting this ratio on a clear downward trend. However, this need not preclude some additional spending in priority areas.[4]

In early 1998, the Minister for Finance will present a new federal budget to Parliament. It is to be expected that the previously-announced cut to the International Assistance Envelope for 1998-99 will be confirmed at that time. However, projected funding for 1999-2000 is not yet known. The tabling of the budget will be a critical moment for the future of Canada's ODA programme. An announcement of a further decline in the International Assistance Envelope would be a fundamental setback to prospects for a recovery in Canada's ODA volume. Even holding the aid budget constant would involve a further decline in ODA/GNP performance. An increase of around 5 per cent (in nominal terms) would be needed simply for Canada's ODA not to lose any further ground in relation to GNP growth.

2

CANADA'S DEVELOPMENT CO-OPERATION INITIATIVES AND PROGRAMMES

A. OVERVIEW OF ROLES AND STRUCTURES IN THE CANADIAN GOVERNMENT

1. Key actors

The **Canadian International Development Agency** is the main instrument for Canada's ODA programme. It is responsible for the management of the International Assistance Envelope and delivers nearly 80 per cent of ODA funded from the Envelope. Table 1 presents details of expected disbursements from the International Assistance Envelope for the 1996-97 and 1997-98 fiscal years. CIDA's President reports to the Minister for International Co-operation, who is also Minister responsible for the Francophonie. Since May 1995, CIDA has taken over responsibility for the delivery of Canada's programme to central and eastern European countries (CEECs) from DFAIT, which still maintains broad policy responsibility in this area.

Other federal bodies are also active in Canada's development co-operation programme. The **Department of Finance** is responsible for Canada's participation in the International Monetary Fund (IMF) and the World Bank. The **Department of Foreign Affairs and International Trade** allocates some grants and contributions to international organisations and the ODA-eligible costs related to the Summits of the Francophonie. Through funding for the **International Development Research Centre (IDRC)**, Canada is helping researchers from developing countries find solutions to social, economic and environmental problems.

A number of other public sector organisations undertake ODA-related activities, including the **International Centre for Human Rights and Democratic Development (ICHRDD)**. A diagram displaying the various federal organisations involved in Canada's programme is given as Chart 1. Further details regarding the responsibilities of these various actors is provided in Chapter 6.

2. Policy coherence and aid co-ordination

"Canadian development assistance initiatives are most effective when they are part of a coherent Canadian approach, based on clearly articulated objectives, solid analysis of events and trends and the co-ordinated use of policy instruments. The impact of CIDA's actions can be blunted when information and analysis are lacking or faulty, when objectives are unclear and when other foreign policy measures work at cross purposes."

[*Human Rights: Government of Canada Policy for CIDA on Human Rights, Democratisation and Good Governance*, December 1995, page 5]

Canada is clearly aware of the importance of policy coherence and has developed structures, both formal and informal, to ensure coherence in its foreign policies, including its relations with developing countries. Given the shared responsibilities for Canadian foreign policies, the International Assistance Envelope and relations with multilateral institutions, collaboration and co-ordination to ensure coherent approaches is important in the Canadian context and is being successfully achieved.

Ministers and Secretaries of State in the foreign policy portfolios and their deputies meet on a regular and as-needed basis to discuss issues and promote policy coherence. At a more formal level, the Minister for International Co-operation circulates as a matter of course decision memoranda to the Minister of Foreign Affairs and the relevant secretaries of state, which indicate whether consultation between CIDA and DFAIT has occurred and the respective views of the two organisations.

Inter-departmental committees are frequently used for consultation, co-ordination of departmental inputs and preparation of common positions. Inter-departmental committees have been formed to prepare for major international events, such as G7 or Francophone summits, Asia-Pacific Economic

Table 1. **Breakdown of International Assistance Envelope**

C$ thousands, cash basis

	1996-97 Main Estimates	1997-98 Main Estimates
Canadian International Development Agency:		
Geographic Programmes	734 718	673 578
Multilateral Programme:		
– Bilateral Food Aid	143 597	119 379
– Multilateral Food Aid	107 693	96 935
– International Humanitarian Assistance and Peacebuilding	73 758	77 178
– International Financial Institutions	162 200	148 201
– Multilateral Technical Co-operation	108 787	104 021
Canadian Partnership Programme		
– Voluntary Sector and Special Projects	208 253	188 194
– Industrial Co-operation	64 956	61 700
– Scholarships	8 900	8 589
Development Information Programme	3 879	3 531
International Centre for Human Rights and Democratic Development	5 000	4 586
Administration	101 000	98 965
Sub-total: CIDA – Official Development Assistance	**1 722 741**	**1 584 857**
Countries in Transition – Programme	101 025	92 630
Countries in Transition – Administration	6 523	6 295
Sub-total: CIDA – Official Development Assistance and Official Aid	**1 830 289**	**1 683 782**
Other Departments and Agencies		
International Financial Institutions (Department of Finance)	237 800	222 800
International Development Research Centre	96 077	88 111
Grants and Contributions (DFAIT)		
– Assessed Contributions	64 309	69 023
– Voluntary Contributions	8 426	9 525
– Scholarships	8 900	8 589
Other Departments and Agencies	2 350	2 350
Administration DFAIT (for services rendered in the field)	33 400	32 230
Sub-total: Other Departments and Agencies – Official Development Assistance	**451 262**	**432 628**
Countries in Transition – Administration (field)	2 477	2 390
Sub-total: Other Departments and Agencies – ODA and Official Aid	**453 739**	**435 018**
Gross Official Development Assistance	**2 174 003**	**2 017 485**
Less repayment of previous years' loans, Green Plan, GEF and translation	64 028	57 800
Net Official Development Assistance	**2 109 975**	**1 959 685**
Official aid	110 025	101 315
TOTAL: INTERNATIONAL ASSISTANCE ENVELOPE	**2 220 000**	**2 061 000**

Note: Canadian fiscal year runs from 1 April to 31 March.
Source: CIDA 1997-98 Estimates Part III – Expenditure Plan.

Co-operation (APEC) or Commonwealth meetings and UN conferences. Other committees are established on a more permanent basis and meet regularly to consider on-going issues. For example, the "monthly expanded trade bureau meeting", which involves representatives from a range of interested departments, is an important mechanism for discussing broader trade-related policy issues. Subsidiary inter-departmental committees are also formed as required to respond to particular issues.

As regards multilateral institutions, the responsible organisation consults with other interested departments and agencies on Canada's position and when developing policies. This is particularly so for the international financial institutions, where the Minister for Finance is Governor for the Bretton Woods institutions and the Minister of Foreign Affairs is Governor for the regional development banks. In consultation with CIDA, the two departments work together in a mutually-reinforcing part-

Chart 1. Aid-related organisations of Federal Government

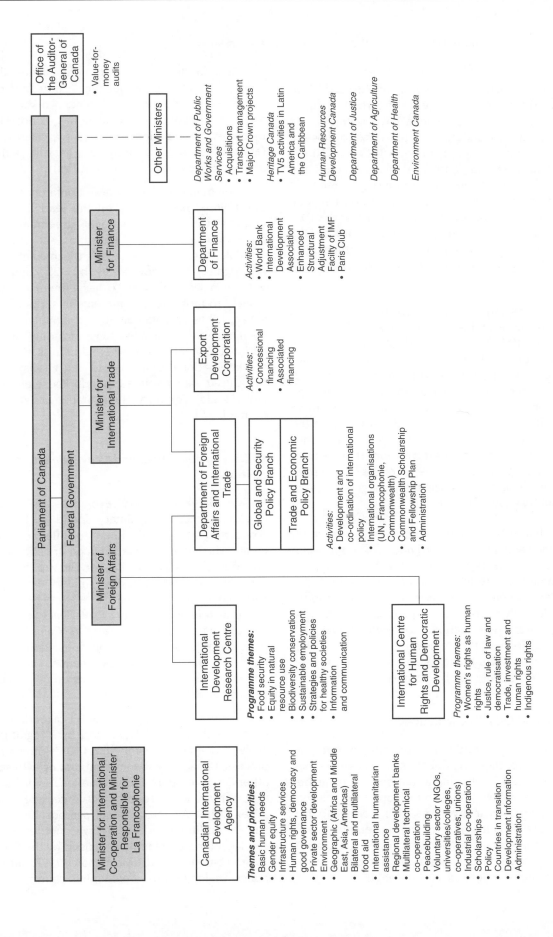

Source: OECD.

nership to co-ordinate positions at the executive boards.

The International Development Research Centre and the International Centre for Human Rights and Democratic Development have different but complementary mandates and functions to those of CIDA. The arm's length status of IDRC and ICHRDD mean that these two Centres can make contacts and take initiatives that the government itself could not do. Liaison and constructive collaboration between IDRC and ICHRDD on the one hand and CIDA, DFAIT and other interested departments on the other has been important for the strengthening of Canada's overall contribution to development co-operation.

Canada's Programme on Governance in South Africa is an example of effective collaboration between CIDA and IDRC and of the benefit of Canada being able to operate through the IDRC when CIDA's role is necessarily more constrained, such as in pre-elections South Africa. Canadians can take pride in the contribution their programme made during the transition period leading up to the first multi-racial democratic elections in South Africa in 1994, when Canadian research support and expert advice strengthened the capacity of the local democratic movement to participate in negotiations on the country's future (see Box 1).

Within CIDA, a number of mechanisms exist for coherence and internal co-ordination. The President and Vice-Presidents, meeting as the Agency's Executive Committee, exercise a co-ordination role. Policy and Management Committees provide an opportunity to identify areas which require or would benefit from greater co-ordination. Country/Regional Programming Frameworks are developed in partnership with the main CIDA branches and with consultations with Canada's civil society partners.

3. Special Canadian initiatives

In line with its traditional commitment to multilateral approaches to global issues, Canada has taken the lead in bringing a number of urgent but politically sensitive issues to the top of the international agenda. In many cases, this leadership has proven critical in mobilising other governments and international public opinion. In all cases, Canada's focus has been on persuasion and dialogue, rather than unilateral actions or confrontation.

Landmines

Canada declared a comprehensive unilateral moratorium on the production, export and operational use of anti-personnel mines (APMs) in January 1996. Subsequently, Canada has disposed of its inventory of landmines except for a small number retained for training purposes (as still permitted under the new treaty banning APMs).

Beginning with the Ottawa Conference in October 1996, Canada has taken the lead in on-going efforts towards an international agreement banning the production, transfer, utilisation and stockpiling of APMs. The "Ottawa Process", which culminated in the signing of a new treaty by 122 countries in Ottawa in December 1997, has proved a powerful vehicle to mobilise governments in support of such a ban. It has complemented and stimulated efforts by humanitarian organisations, including the International Commission of the Red Cross (ICRC) and the International Campaign to Ban Landmines and the ICRC to rally public support for these efforts on a global scale. (See also "Humanitarian assistance and de-mining" below.)

Military expenditures and Conventional arms control

Canada in the World recognises the negative impact of excessive military spending, calling for "concerted action with others to influence governments which spend large sums on arms rather than on education and housing for their people" and "assisting societies to reduce military expenditures and reconstruct civil societies". A strategy document entitled *Reduction of Military Expenditures in Developing Countries* establishing the basis for Canadian initiatives in this area was tabled in Parliament in June 1996. It identifies development co-operation as one instrument available for fostering peace and security in developing countries.

Canada has been pursuing this agenda through multilateral policy dialogue and by integrating the analysis of human security into CIDA's programming process. Canada has been collaborating with several other DAC Members and international organisations to examine ways to address excessive military expenditure. An international symposium on Military Expenditures in Developing Countries, Security and Development, jointly organised by the DAC and Canada and held in Ottawa in March 1997, initiated a policy dialogue with developing country officials

Box 1. **South Africa/Canada Programme on Governance**

Prior to our first democratic elections in April 1994, the IDRC played a critical role in helping the African National Congress and the Mass Democratic Movement to prepare for negotiations and it supported us generously in the process. Given its foresight and confidence in the future, the IDRC was instrumental also in helping us prepare for the new phase of governance and transformation. "

Nelson Mandela, President of the Republic of South Africa

The origin of Canada's involvement with South Africa on governance issues goes back to June 1990. Nelson Mandela, while on a visit to Canada shortly after his release from prison, asked the then Prime Minister Brian Mulroney for assistance to help the African National Congress (ANC) understand economic issues better and to develop the ANC's economic policy-making capacity. Canada responded through the IDRC, which brought together a team of international experts to work with the ANC. The IDRC subsequently sponsored similar missions to examine the policy areas of urban planning, science and technology, and the environment. Each mission published policy recommendations which served as the basis for the policies of the new democratic government formed after the 1994 elections.

Another component of Canadian assistance during the pre-election period was the Public Service Policy Project. This project developed from a request made by Nelson Mandela in 1992 for Canadian help to level the playing field by preparing the ANC to participate in negotiations on governance during the period leading up to national elections in 1994. After visiting South Africa, a team from CIDA formulated project proposals in the areas of education policy, macro-economic policy and public administration. IDRC was chosen as the executing agency. One feature of all of the project components was the involvement of senior people, both Canadians and South Africans, for policy formulation and capacity development in these three areas. With respect to the public administration component, a number of close personal relationships were formed between senior South African and Canadian officials that still continue today. The project included a wide range of capacity-building activities designed for South Africans to enable them to participate in government.

The Public Service Policy Project addressed three areas: national government; establishment of provincial governments; and initial staffing of the National Assembly and Provincial Legislative Assemblies. Activities included:

- **Workshops** on key governance issues and the powers, functions and functioning of provincial government;
- **Work attachments** with the Governments of Canada, Namibia or Zimbabwe for 90 future middle- and senior-level managers, as well as a programme of attachments to the Assembly in Zimbabwe, Canada's House of Commons, Ontario's Legislative Assembly and the South African Parliament in Capetown for six candidates for positions in the national or provincial assemblies;
- **Training programmes** for potential foreign affairs officers with the Centre for Foreign Relations in Tanzania (50 candidates) and the Zimbabwean Ministry of Foreign Affairs (25 candidates);
- **Familiarisation visits** to Canadian provinces for ANC candidates for provincial Premiership positions (see below); and
- Provision of **expert advice** on constitutional and governmental matters.

The familiarisation visits as part of this project have led to a number of "twinnings" of South African and Canadian provinces. Initially, short visits to Canada were organised for three ANC candidates for provincial Premier positions. Each candidate was twinned with the Premier of a Canadian Province and visited that Premier's Office and the offices of the legislative assembly, cabinet, cabinet committees, deputy ministers and other senior officials in the province. Twinnings were organised between Saskatchewan and the Free State, and New Brunswick and Northern Cape. These visits were acclaimed as outstanding successes by the South Africans.

The Canadian Premiers and their South African counterparts agreed to maintain twinning relationships after the 1994 South African elections, to allow exchanges to occur to the benefit of the South African provinces during their formative stages and, in the longer term, to the mutual benefit of both Canadian and South African provinces. Since the 1994 elections, other twinning arrangements have been established and are being supported by CIDA. Agreements have been made between Alberta and Mpumalanga, between British Columbia and Eastern Cape, and between Manitoba and North West Province. Visits and exchanges are now taking place at a range of levels. Some recent activities include:

- The Deputy Premier of **Saskatchewan** accompanied a trade delegation to the Free State.
- The new Free State Premier visited **Saskatchewan** and met the Premier, several cabinet ministers and senior officials to discuss the functions and structures of executive government.

(continued on next page)

(continued)

- A Senior Analyst from "Service New Brunswick" visited Northern Cape to work on developing plans for a one-stop service delivery system, based on the **New Brunswick** model.
- The Secretary to the **New Brunswick** Cabinet visited Northern Cape to work on issues related to the functioning of cabinet and executive decision making. While there, she conducted workshops for the Provincial Cabinet as well as for the heads of provincial departments.
- The Premier of Mpumalanga led a trade mission to **Alberta**.
- In response to a request from the Mpumalanga's Premier's Office, the **Alberta** Chief of Protocol and Director of Multilateral Relations visited Mpumalanga to assist with the development of their Protocol Office and intergovernmental relations.
- Four officials from **Manitoba** visited North Western Province and worked on organisational structure and strategy with the Departments of Agriculture and Economic Development, reorganisation of the Director-General's Office and support for the development of the Internal Audit function.
- The Premier of **Manitoba** visited North West Province. During a follow-up trade mission, several joint venture operations were formed.

Box 10 provides further details of CIDA's Bilateral Programme to South Africa.

---

and experts and helped promote consensus on a multilateral agenda for action in this area.

Canada is also active in raising the profile of excessive military expenditures as an economic development, public expenditure management and good governance issue at the international level – including at the G7 Summits of Halifax and Lyon, the Annual Meetings of the IMF and World Bank; various donor co-ordination fora and the Commonwealth and the Francophonie. This has included encouraging the IMF, the World Bank and the OECD to play a central role in data collection and analysis in the area of military expenditures and supporting, with other donors and the DAC, the preparation of regional studies on the impact of military expenditures on security and the prospects of sustainable development. The result of this analysis is beginning to be taken into account in the formulation of country programmes and policy dialogue with developing country partners.

Canada is active in promoting greater transparency in conventional arms trade, including through the Convention of Certain Conventional Weapons, and is a founding contributor to the UN Register of Conventional Arms. Canada is also a founding member of the Wassenaar Arrangement, established in 1995 to seek to ensure regional and international security by preventing destabilizing accumulations of conventional weapons and dual use equipment. Since 1990, DFAIT has issued an Annual Report on the Export of Military Goods from Canada.

Canada has been active in the UN, particularly the UN Disarmament Commission, in promoting recognition of the link between, on the one hand, disarmament (particularly of small arms and light weapons), demobilisation and reintegration of ex-combatants with, on the other hand, social and economic development in post-conflict situations. Canada has also been active in promoting efforts to address the negative consequences in certain areas of the world resulting from excessive and destabilizing accumulations of small arms and light weapons. Canada continues to press forward with "like-minded" countries to promote progress in these areas.

Child labour

Canada has joined Norway's initiative in the fight against the worst forms of child labour and all forms of commercial sexual abuse of children. The Minister of Foreign Affairs has appointed an Advisor for Children's Rights, to help formulate Canada's approach in this high priority area. Recognising that poverty and an absence of adequate social support systems, especially access to good education, push children into exploitative labour, Canada seeks to address this issue through co-operation and dialogue with developing country partners, rather than through trade sanctions or other punitive measures.

Canada is consequently actively encouraging the development by the International Labour Organisation of a new convention focusing on the most hazardous and exploitative forms of child labour, in preparation for adoption at the International Labour Conferences in 1998 and 1999.

Canada is working with "like-minded" countries to ensure successful adoption of the Optional Protocol to the Rights of the Child concerning the sale of children, child pornography and child prostitution. It contributed to and endorsed the Declaration and Agenda for Action at the Conference on Commercial Sexual Exploitation of Children held in Stockholm in August 1996. Canada participated actively in the Conference on Child Labour, held in Oslo in October 1997.

Knowledge and information

With an increasing recognition that access to knowledge is crucial to development, Canada has been active in supporting developing countries working to develop their knowledge sectors and foster wider access to information and communications technologies. Together with the World Bank, the Government of Canada co-hosted a major international conference on harnessing knowledge and information for international development in Toronto in June 1997. "GK97" brought together governments, business people, educators, non-profit institutions, development organisations, scientists and others. Both in Toronto and in the simultaneous virtual conference, GK97 explored the potentials and pitfalls in harnessing the global information revolution in the pursuit of sustainable development – for example, making more cost-effective the delivery of essential services such as health care, education, and natural resource management; improving local governance and promoting human rights; and enabling developing countries to become full partners in the global economy.

The fight against corruption

Canada views transparency and accountability as critical elements of good governance and determining elements of efforts to create an environment conducive to sustainable and equitable economic growth. A widespread belief among the Canadian public that a significant proportion of funds devoted to international co-operation do not reach their intended beneficiaries has also been identified among the principal factors behind the weakening of

support for aid. For example, in partnership with Transparency International, CIDA is working to formulate an initiative in this field.

B. MAIN FEATURES OF CIDA'S POLICIES AND PROGRAMMES

1. Geographical distribution

Canada has widespread and diverse geographic interests, reflecting a unique combination of cultural, demographic and geopolitical factors. It has considerable interests in the Asia-Pacific region, Africa and the Middle East. As a country of the American hemisphere, Canada's economic and political relations with the countries of Latin America are also growing. A member of the Commonwealth, the Francophonie, the Organisation of American States and the Asia-Pacific Economic Co-operation (APEC) forum, Canada maintains relations with a large number of countries. A regional breakdown of Canadian bilateral aid is presented in Table 2.

Over 120 countries receive development assistance from Canada, the 20 largest beneficiaries receiving some two-thirds of Canada's allocable bilateral ODA. The question of a wide geographical dispersion and the need for greater concentration on a limited number of countries is a long-standing issue for the Canadian aid programme. The issue was raised at the last two DAC Reviews in 1990 and 1994, it was one of the main points of the Auditor-General's 1993 Report on CIDA's bilateral programme and is addressed in both *Canada in the World* and *Sharing our Future*. For Canada, it has been and will continue to be a challenge to reconcile both diminishing resources and a widening range of development activities with a vocation to be present and active in most parts of the world. To maximise its developmental impacts, Canada needs to address more energetically its *Canada in the World* commitment "to [focus its] efforts on a limited number of countries, while maintaining programmes in other countries through low-cost, administratively-simple delivery mechanisms" [*Canada in the World*, page 45].

2. Poverty reduction

Poverty reduction is the central focus of CIDA's programming. CIDA's *Policy On Poverty Reduction*, released in January 1996, commits CIDA to contribute through its programmes to a "sustained reduction in the number of people living in poverty in developing countries, and in the extent of their

Table 2. **Breakdown of Canadian bilateral official development assistance**

Percentages, two-year averages

	1990/91	1995/96
Sub-Saharan Africa	23.6	18.7
North Africa and Middle East	5.4	8.1
Asia	19.5	14.0
America	8.7	7.9
Oceania	0.0	0.0
Europe	0.1	1.5
Geographically allocated	57.3	50.1
Geographically unallocated (includes ODA through NGOs, scholarships and imputed student costs, costs of maintaining refugees and administrative costs)	42.7	49.9
Bilateral ODA	100.0	100.0
For reference:		
Bilateral ODA at 1995 prices and exchange rates	$1 555	$1 358

Source: OECD.

deprivation". The policy also aims to provide a unifying theme for all of CIDA's programming and an analytical link with the six ODA priorities. In the context of programmes and projects not directly targeted at the poor, it calls for a systematic analysis of distributional effects, in order to minimise direct or indirect negative impacts on the poor and, where possible, the identification of opportunities for complementary activities which could benefit the poor.

For analytical purposes, the policy classifies poverty reduction activities as follows:

- **targeted poverty reduction activities** are those which work directly with the poor to improve their welfare;

- **poverty-focused activities** comprise programmes and activities which benefit the poor but do not involve working directly with them; and

- **policy-level interventions** comprise activities which affect the policy environment in such a way as to address the root causes of poverty, by helping remove systemic constraints at both national and international levels.

While these categories are analytically distinct, CIDA recognises that programming often encompasses more than one category, and that an appropriate policy environment is necessary for activities to be effective. CIDA believes its resources can have maximum impact by concentrating on "poverty-focused" and "policy-level" activities.

A preliminary review of implementation of the *Policy on Poverty Reduction* identified the need to

develop and disseminate guidelines and methodological tools and techniques to help CIDA staff implement the poverty mandate at the operational level. It also pointed to the need for statistical indicators and benchmark data in order to monitor the implementation of the policy, in line with CIDA's results-based management approach. A formal evaluation of the policy is to be conducted before June 2000.

3. Programme priorities

Canada in the World sets out six programme priorities for Canadian ODA: basic human needs; women in development; infrastructures services; human rights, democracy and good governance; private sector development; and environment. These represent a clear shift away from a sector focus towards results-based programming. The six programme priorities now form the basis of CIDA's reporting on its activities, and in 1994 a system was put in place to track disbursements by priority. However, the coding, counting and classification systems need some refinement and the accuracy of current reporting is considered to be somewhat imperfect. CIDA is making significant efforts in this priority area.

Taken together, CIDA's programme priorities represent a formidable agenda for any agency to take on. It is not the intention for each of CIDA's country and other programmes to address all these challenges simultaneously. While environmental impact and gender equality are treated by CIDA as fundamental cross-cutting concerns that are addressed in all activities, the objective for CIDA's geographical branches is to formulate coherent programmes consistent with one or more priorities in line with the needs and circumstances of partner countries and to complement activities of other donors. The definition of measurable and realistic objectives, consistent with available financial and human resources, is another key challenge.

Over the past few years, considerable progress has been made towards formulating policies and procedures to guide programming in support of these priorities, as discussed below. There is evidence, however, of a need for greater clarity with regard to the concrete implications of some of these policies as well as their relative weights in particular activities in specific countries. Examples include the distinction between the poverty reduction and basic human needs concepts and priorities, and the importance of private sector development and infrastructure services relative to some of the other priorities.

The development or refinement of tools and techniques to allow a qualitative monitoring of the impact of CIDA activities towards these priorities is another area for further work in the future.

Basic human needs

Canada is committed to providing 25 per cent of its ODA to basic human needs which includes emergency humanitarian assistance. In 1996-97, CIDA's ODA programme expenditures for basic human needs were 38.4 per cent, including food aid and humanitarian assistance (33.9 per cent excluding emergency humanitarian aid). Other government bodies, which account for a quarter of Canada's gross ODA expenditures, do not report their basic human needs disbursements.

CIDA's *Policy on Meeting Basic Human Needs*, approved in March 1997, builds on principles from the 1995 World Summit for Social Development in Copenhagen and the *Shaping the 21st Century* Strategy. The policy recognises that developing countries have principal responsibility for meeting the basic human needs of people living in poverty in their country and places particular emphasis on sustainability.

Specific activities in the area of basic human needs include support for the provision of primary health care, basic education, family planning, nutrition, water and sanitation, and shelter as well as emergency humanitarian assistance to victims of natural or human-induced disasters.

In this context, CIDA is also paying special attention to addressing the needs of children, including programmes of income-generation, primary education and child-care (particularly for girls), strengthening the position of women, and the protection of the rights of children. In 1994-95, the Asia, Africa and Middle East and Americas Branches allocated more than 20 per cent of their disbursements for projects of direct benefit to children. These focused on child and maternal health, nutrition, immunisation and basic education.

Human rights, democracy and good governance

The Government of Canada regards respect for human rights not only as a fundamental value, but also as a crucial element in the development of stable, democratic and prosperous societies at peace with each other. Its approach to rights, democracy and governance emphasizes civil society organisations as key vehicles for articulating popular concerns and channelling popular participation in decision and policy making. Another key focus is on the responsibility of governments to manage public affairs in an honest, effective and accountable manner.

The Government of Canada Policy for CIDA *on Human Rights, Democratisation and Good Governance*, adopted in December 1995, acknowledges that the development perspective articulated by CIDA is not the only interest to be reflected in Canadian foreign policy – political and commercial interests are also important. While the Department of Foreign Affairs and International Trade has the lead role in establishing the basic parameters for integrating these themes into the overall foreign policy context, CIDA is responsible for the formulation of programmes relating to human rights and good governance. The policy also mandates CIDA to ensure effective policy co-ordination with Departments such as Defence, Finance and Environment and other organisations in the public sector, including ICHRDD, IDRC and the Export Development Corporation

In serious human rights situations, Canada's policy is to use all possible means to maintain co-operation in order to work for change with the government and civil society. This aims to avoid hurting even more those suffering from abuses. In such circumstances, the emphasis is to work towards co-ordinated multilateral approaches. This is in line with Canada's long-standing policy of emphasizing constructive dialogue and avoiding punitive measures, where possible.

CIDA has made remarkable headway in the area of human rights and democracy. Activities in this area have been growing rapidly over the past few years, despite restrictions in the ODA budget. In 1995-96, they accounted for over C$ 45 million, allocated over some 400 projects, about 10.5 per cent of total disbursements. These have focused on strengthening democratic processes and the rule of law, supporting the role of civil society and human rights organisations, and promoting dialogue and mediation to avoid social conflicts (see Box 2).

Country development policy framework documents and institutional support strategies now include explicit objectives for rights, democracy and governance programming, as illustrated in the case of China, with whom CIDA co-operates in areas such as women's rights, labour laws, criminal law, employment equity and public accounting and auditing.

CIDA is also called upon to provide support for the Government of Canada's response to urgent human rights situations. Priority countries of focus include Haiti, Rwanda, Sri Lanka, South Africa, Guatemala, El Salvador and China. A recent example is CIDA's financial support for the training of Haitian civilian police in the context of broader efforts in support of peacebuilding and democratisation.

A review of CIDA's programming experience in the area of human rights and governance, completed in 1996, pointed to the need for CIDA to develop programming guidelines and performance monitoring and evaluation tools in the areas of human rights and democratic development, and to build in-house analytical expertise to provide technical advice to the field and programme branches operating in these relatively high-risk fields of activity.

Women in development and gender equity

The priority accorded to this objective in Canada's ODA is based on the government's long-standing commitment to gender equity within Canadian society. The Federal Plan for Gender Equality (Canada's submission to the 1995 United Nations Fourth World Conference on Women in Beijing) identifies the promotion of gender equality at the global level as a Canadian government priority and commits the government to pursue gender equality objectives in multilateral fora and organisations.

Box 2. **Governance, Human Rights and Democracy: CIDA Activities**

CIDA programmes in the area of governance, human rights and democracy involve a large variety of partner organisations, including educational institutions, professional organisations, and non-governmental organisations (NGOs) in developing countries and in Canada. These activities can be grouped into four broad categories:

- strengthening **democratic processes**: this includes support for democratic institutions such as legislatures; support for the development of electoral processes, including voter education campaigns; and the provision of electoral observers;

- building **the rule of law** and strengthening **human rights institutions**: this includes training of judges and paralegal workers, dissemination of statutes and law reports; and strengthening human rights commissions and ombudsman offices;

- **strengthening civil society**: this includes building the capacity for independent social, economic and political analysis, through training and international networking; and

- helping to **resolve social conflict, strengthen dialogue and build the role of the media**: these activities include support for the reform of police and security forces; support for mediation initiatives; and efforts to build an independent, responsible media through technical assistance and linkages between journalists.

CIDA's *Policy on Women in Development and Gender Equity*, updated in 1995 following an extensive review process, moves beyond a focus on equal treatment to embrace the concept of gender equity. It requires all development initiatives, whether at the macro-policy or project level, to include gender analysis and, if required, special measures to facilitate women's participation. It calls for specific efforts to monitor and evaluate the impact of CIDA-supported policies and programmes on women. In operational terms, CIDA distinguishes between "integrated" and "specific" WID actions:

- **WID-integrated** efforts refer to activities where an understanding of gender differences has been incorporated into overall planning and activities. The goal, objectives and delivery mechanisms are aimed at women's needs, interests and participation as much as men's. In 1995-96, an estimated one-third of CIDA's bilateral programme was "WID-integrated".

• **WID-specific** efforts are those which target women exclusively. In 1995-96, CIDA disbursements for this priority represented 3.2 per cent of total disbursements

Specific guidelines have been developed to foster inclusion of gender considerations in country/regional programming frameworks, highlighting the importance of sex-disaggregated data and gender analysis. Within the context of results-based management, project and programme level results for WID and gender equity are to be reported on annually as part of the normal Agency reporting.

Preliminary results from a major review of the Agency's WID and gender equity activities, initiated in 1995, point to a growing commitment to WID and gender equity within the Agency. They also highlight a need for further strengthening, notably with regard to the establishment of measurable targets for WID and gender equity programming.

Infrastructure services

Traditionally, support in this area has focused on the energy, transport, water and telecommunications sectors. In recent years, emphasis has been shifting towards building the necessary capacity in planning and managing the delivery of infrastructures services and on equitable access to these services. This includes assistance for the development of a policy, regulatory and legal environment conducive to private sector participation in the financing of infrastructure development. In 1995-96, CIDA disbursements for this priority represented 13.6 per cent of total disbursements. A policy for infrastructure services is to be developed in early 1998.

Private sector development

Canada recognises the vital role that the private sector can play in pursuit of sustainable development and poverty reduction. As in the case of infrastructure services, CIDA's approach to private sector development focuses on creating the conditions conducive to private sector investment in productive activities, through reforming the regulatory and legal framework, and building human and institutional capacity for economic management.

Other priorities include building linkages between the Canadian private sector and those of developing-country partners, strengthening entrepreneurial capacity and providing support to local enterprises, including through micro-credit. Through its Industrial Co-operation Programme (INC), CIDA is directly involved in establishing Canadian private sector presence in key emerging markets considered too risky by both commercial creditors and the Export Development Corporation (see Chapter 4). In 1995-96, CIDA disbursements for private sector development as a whole represented 10.4 per cent of total disbursements.

Environment

Canada is committed to helping developing countries protect their environment and contribute to addressing global and regional environmental issues. Examples of activities in this area include the Environment Management and Development Project in Indonesia, which since its inception in 1983 has played an important role in strengthening Indonesia's planning and institutional base for the sustainable development of its natural resources, and the China Council for International Co-operation on Environment and Development (CCICED) (see Box 3).

CIDA's *Policy on Environmental Sustainability* was adopted in 1992 in preparation for the United Nations Conference on Environment and Development in Rio de Janeiro.[5] It focuses on strengthening the capability of developing countries to contribute to the resolution of global and regional environmental problems, while meeting their development objectives. In 1995-96, CIDA disbursements for this priority represented 7.4 per cent of total disbursements. Following adoption of the policy, CIDA programming in the area of environmental management has increased sharply, with a notable emphasis on capacity development for environmental management.

An independent review of CIDA efforts in the field of environment concluded in 1995 pointed to the need for further progress with regard to the integration of environmental issues in the context of country programming, with a view to improving overall sustainability. The development of CIDA's new information data base and the inclusion of environmental impact assessment (EIA) control protocols on the Agency-wide information system is expected to lead to improvements in this regard (see Box 4).

Box 3. **China Council for International Co-operation on Environment and Development**

With CIDA playing a leading role, the China Council for International Co-operation on Environment and Development was set up in 1992 as a high-level consultative organisation to strengthen co-operation and exchange between China and the international community in the field of environment and development. It is a capacity building organisation, aiming to provide information and recommendations to China's State Council about important problems that China faces. CCICED operates through a series of Working Groups on a number of themes, including energy strategy and technology; pollution control; environmental economics; biodiversity protection; trade and environment; and sustainable agriculture and cleaner industrial production.

CCICED's executive is led by the Chair of the Environmental Protection Commission of China's State Council, assisted by three Vice-Chairs, including the President of CIDA. The National Environmental Protection Agency (NEPA) has been designated as the Chinese organisation responsible for the CCICED and has established a small secretariat for the Council. A Canadian Support Office at Simon Fraser University in Vancouver manages donor contributions, recommends international experts and works with the NEPA secretariat to support the Council.

CIDA has always been the "lead" donor to the CCICED, but the project involves other international organisations and agencies. To date, direct financial support has also been contributed by the British Department for International Development, the Ford Foundation, the Rockefeller Foundation, the German Agency for Technical Co -operation, the Netherlands' Environment Ministry and the Ministry of International Trade and Industry of Japan. In addition, the World Bank, UNDP and the Asian Development Bank also support the work of the Council.

An example of CCICED activities is the Working Group on Trade and Environment, which was established in January 1995 and is co-chaired by NEPA and Canada's International Institute for Sustainable Development (IISD). This Working Group aims to assist China in developing and implementing long-term, comprehensive and integrated trade and environment policies and measures that are supportive of sustainable development. It is active in four key areas:

- examining possibilities for joint implementation of greenhouse gas mitigation measures;
- promoting measures to restrict the use of ozone-depleting substances in foreign direct investments;
- examining potential sources of green protectionism in developed country markets, in particular the effects of eco-labelling and voluntary environmental standards (including ISO 14000); and
- accelerating "Greenfood" (ecologically labelled food) development in China.

The Working Group has presented recommendations on all these issues.

---

4. Other important CIDA activities

Conflict prevention and peacebuilding

Canada views peacebuilding as the effort to restore human security and foster a return to peace and stability in countries which have fallen into conflict. This comprises two mutually-supporting approaches: short-term diplomatic and political initiatives, to help countries emerge from violent conflict to implement political and military peace accords; and long-term efforts, to build local capacity to address the root causes of conflict, strengthen indigenous conflict resolution mechanisms and foster the emergence of participatory political structures conducive to a culture of peace. A note on peacebuilding, human rights, democracy and good governance is given in Box 5.

CIDA has traditionally responded to the needs of countries in conflict by integrating peacebuilding activities into its long-term development efforts. CIDA has provided funding in support of projects to re-integrate uprooted populations and refugees, support dialogue and reconciliation between conflictive groups, strengthen regional conflict management institutions and other activities related to peacebuilding. CIDA is also working to develop project evaluation procedures aimed at ensuring that development initiatives in countries prone to violent conflict integrate and support peacebuilding objectives.

Box 4. **Environmental Impact Assessment**

The dismantling of the Professional Services Branch, as part of CIDA's Agency-wide reorganisation, resulted in the redeployment of environmental expertise throughout the Agency. However, a centralised environmental impact assessment unit, the Environmental Assessment and Compliance Unit was subsequently established within CIDA's Policy Branch to oversee the implementation of the Canadian Environmental Assessment Act of 1995. This legislation requires projects receiving federal funding to be subjected to an environmental review. Within the geographical programme branches, accountability for conducting environmental assessments lies with project managers. EIA requirements have also been integrated into the Bilateral Road Map for the various business lines that comprise CIDA programming. Specific EIA guides are being formulated for each business line. The quality of EIA performed in connection with CIDA supported projects is considered to be good, perhaps helped by the introduction of EIA as a legal requirement. The Canadian Partnership Branch is in the process of determining legal implications of delegating authority for compliance with the Canadian Environmental Assessment Act to partner organisations. The principle underlying such a delegation would be complete compliance with the terms of the Act.

A new development is the Canadian Peacebuilding Initiative, co-sponsored by DFAIT and CIDA. This initiative aims to speed up responses to crises through more co-ordinated and coherent approaches, drawing on the full range of government and non-governmental expertise. It includes an inter-departmental planning mechanism led by DFAIT and CIDA and a formal consultation process to co-ordinate policies, programmes, priorities and strategies that support conflict prevention and peacebuilding and advise ministers on actions that Canada could take. The initiative aims to mobilise the peacebuilding expertise of Canadian NGOs, academic institutions, religious and professional associations.

This new initiative also includes the establishment of a Peacebuilding Fund, with a C$ 20 million budget to be provided by CIDA over the period 1997-99. This is designed as a rapid-response mechanism to support urgent peace initiatives, often

seen as an essential complement to the long-term support provided by development co-operation programmes. It includes support for peace accords and local peace dialogues, strengthening locally-generated peacebuilding initiatives, as well as enhancing governance and civil society. Recently, the Fund was used to provide support for a peace mission conducted by a special representative of the Secretary-General of the UN and the Organisation of African Unity to find a peaceful solution to the conflicts in the Great Lakes region of Africa. The Fund has also supported the establishment of Guatemala's Historical Clarification Commission, mandated to look into human rights violations committed during the 35-year long civil war in Guatemala. Canada, as the first country to contribute, has been a catalyst for other donors in participating in this initiative.

Canada has played a leading role in the formulation of the DAC *Guidelines on Conflict, Peace and Development Co-operation*, endorsed by the DAC High-Level Meeting in May 1997.

Humanitarian assistance and de-mining

CIDA's International Humanitarian Assistance (IHA) Programme is the Canadian government's principal conduit for non-food emergency humanitarian assistance to developing countries. IHA funds emergency response activities in the areas of water and sanitation, temporary housing, repatriation, reintegration, demobilization and mine-related activities. Associated logistics and administration costs may also be eligible for funding. There is no requirement to purchase relief supplies in Canada.

IHA channels its funds through organisations and agencies of the United Nations (66 per cent in 1995-96), the Red Cross Movement (23 per cent) and Canadian NGOs with proven capacity in emergency assistance (11 per cent). Appeals for emergency support are assessed in consultation with the concerned Canadian mission overseas, relevant programmes in CIDA and DFAIT.

About half of the IHA expenditures are allocated to Africa. The Rwanda tragedy accounted for 25 per cent of total IHA disbursements in 1994-95 as well as for an increase in programme expenditure from C$ 90.6 million to C$ 105.4 million.

Canada recognises that de-mining is often a precondition for the provision of humanitarian assistance and longer-term social and economic recon-

---

Box 5. **Peacebuilding, Human Rights, Democracy and Good Governance**

A *note by the Dutch Examiners*

Over the past two years, Canada has made important progress in adapting its international assistance policies to support conflict prevention and peacebuilding. An intensive dialogue among the Department of Foreign Affairs and International Trade, the Department of National Defence, CIDA and Canadian NGOs, examined shortcomings in the handling of so-called humanitarian emergency situations in developing countries.

The Review team found that the consultation mechanism of establishing *ad hoc* working groups for policy dialogue on key issues and countries with the active participation of all relevant country and/or thematic branches of DFAIT, CIDA, Defence and IDRC, as appropriate, has in a substantive way contributed to the identification of lessons, their incorporation in a coherent, broad policy framework, and the operationalisation of new policies for conflict prevention and peacebuilding. Issues of broad policy coherence are led by the policy branches of DFAIT and CIDA.

This coherent, broad approach reflects a high level of integration between a variety of development co-operation policies, such as humanitarian assistance in emergency situations; longer-term development co-operation aiming at poverty reduction, equity and sustainable economic growth; and so-called "soft sectors" such as human rights, democratisation and good governance.

In this respect, CIDA's efforts to link longer-term development issues with new and innovative approaches towards conflict prevention which go beyond the traditional realm of development co-operation are of particular interest and require a high level of co-ordination with other departments in the international portfolios. Among the issues where Canada has made significant progress, and which are considered by the Review team as being important components of a broad, integrated policy towards peacebuilding and conflict prevention, are the following:

- the analysis of the root causes of violent conflicts in developing countries;
- the establishment of linkages with shorter-term preventive diplomacy and politico-military orientations;
- the promotion by CIDA of interventions in the areas of human rights, democratisation and good governance, which are fundamental in themselves and essential conditions for peace and development;
- the Canadian Peacebuilding Initiative and the establishment of a Peacebuilding Fund;
- the Canadian initiative to improve the capacity of the UN to get peacekeepers more rapidly into the field in response to emerging crises;
- the Canadian initiative to arrive at a global ban on anti-personnel mines;
- Canada's ongoing efforts within international fora over the past two years to promote the reduction of military expenditures in those developing countries where these are excessive;
- CIDA's practice to integrate the issue of excessive military expenditure into the development co-operation dialogue with partners to encourage productive resource allocation; and
- Canada's efforts to promote greater transparency in the trade of military goods, which is well reflected in its own annual reports issued by DFAIT (showing military exports by country of destination and category according to the Export Control List).

---

struction. Since 1993-94, CIDA has provided C$ 12 million in support for landmine removal and victim assistance in several countries, mainly in the context of UN-led multisectoral humanitarian assistance programmes. Such programmes generally include mine awareness training for civilians to identify and avoid APMs, increasing their individual safety; mine education for children, including mine identification and safe behaviour; and mine removal training for local mine clearance personnel. In the case of Angola, Canada's early support and financial

assistance served to build up support for these programmes among other donors.

Food aid

Canada's food aid volume has declined considerably over the past five years and its share in total food aid has dropped from around 9 per cent in 1990 to around 5 per cent in 1996. Canada's combined bilateral and multilateral food aid budget, which had declined from C$ 306 million to

C$ 256 million in 1995-96 is scheduled to fall further, to around C$ 200 million in 1998-99. Thus, Canadian food aid has diminished considerably more than the overall ODA budget.

Following significant increases in emergency food aid and long-term refugee food support over the period 1993 to 1995, the trend has been reversed and emergency food aid now accounts for under 40 per cent of the total. The share of non-emergency food aid allocated to least-developed countries rose from 55 per cent in 1993-94 to 74 per cent in 1997-98. The share of non-emergency food aid funds targeted to specific poor groups rose from 49 per cent to 83 per cent over the same period.

The qualitative shifts have been striking, with a re-orientation of Canada's Food Aid Strategy towards poverty reduction. The priority is now on using food aid as an investment in human capital targeted at the most needy, notably poor women and children. Bilateral food aid programmes are thus to form an integral part of CIDA country strategies and assistance programmes, subjected to the same results-based assessment. In addition to ensuring that food aid does not disrupt local markets or discourage local production, it includes using specially targetted food-for-work programmes to improve the nutritional status of women and children, or to act as an incentive for vulnerable populations to attend health clinics for immunisation and other primary health services.

Another critical innovation is a focus on addressing qualitative nutritional deficiencies, through the direct provision of micronutrient supplements (vitamins and minerals). These now account for about 16 per cent of the total value of non-emergency food aid allocations. This is fully in line with research findings in the field of nutrition and the approaches being promoted by the World Food Programme. The UN Children's Fund (UNICEF) estimated that Canada's contribution to its efforts against iodine deficiency had saved three million children in 1995 from mental impairment due to iodine deficiency.

Through CIDA and IDRC, Canada is also the main sponsor of the Micronutrient Initiative which aims to facilitate the global fight against malnutrition, through advocacy, research, information dissemination, programming and networking activities. Other sponsors of this initiative include the World Bank, UNICEF, United Nations Development Programme (UNDP) and the United States Agency for International Development.

C.   MULTILATERAL AID

Canada's views its support to multilateral organisations as critical to both its foreign policy and its development co-operation objectives, and as an essential complement to its bilateral approaches. While Canada has traditionally had a much higher level of multilateral contributions as a share of ODA than the DAC average, this leadership position has been eroding. There have been reductions in Canada's participation in a number of special multilateral funds and Canada's share in the most recent replenishment of the Asian Development Fund was reduced from 7.3 per cent to 4.6 per cent and in the African Development Fund from 8.3 per cent to 4.5 per cent. Canadian contributions to the World Food Programme have also declined considerably since 1994.

These reductions, which bring Canada's contributions in line with its relative weight in the global economy, reflect budget constraints rather than any apparent erosion of commitment to multilateralism. Canada continues to take its participation in multilateral organisations very seriously, committing major intellectual resources and devoting considerable efforts to influence the overall policy directions and programming of the multilateral development organisations to which it belongs. Canada has also been expressing its concern regarding the weakening of traditional "burden-sharing" practices used to fund multilateral development institutions and has sought to encourage increased participation by non-traditional donors.

Although it now finds itself in a somewhat weaker position, Canada retains an active role in the major international financial institutions (IFIs), including the IMF, the World Bank and the Regional Development Banks. Table 3 shows Canada's share of contributions to multilateral development banks.

At the IMF, Canada's priority is to ensure that lending facilities and policies are adapted to cope with the emerging needs of the world economy and can deal with potential crises. The 1995 Halifax G7 Summit recommended a number of reforms to the IMF's procedures and facilities and Canada is supporting efforts to address these issues. Canada sees the challenge ahead for the IMF as the need to obtain sufficient resources to support both its regular lending operations and the Enhanced Structural Adjustment Facility for heavily-indebted poor countries (HIPC).

Table 3. **Canada's share in multilateral development banks**

Percentages

	As of 31 December 1992	As of 31 December 1996
Cumulative capital subscriptions		
International Bank for Reconstruction and Development	3.3	3.0[1]
Inter-American Development Bank	4.4	4.2
Asian Development Bank	5.8	5.4
African Development Bank	3.3	3.2
Caribbean Development Bank	10.4	10.4
European Bank for the Reconstruction and Development	3.5	3.4
Share of most recent concessional fund replenishments		
International Development Association	4.0	3.8
Fund for Special Operations (Inter-American Development Bank)	5.5	5.5
Asian Development Fund	7.3	4.7
African Development Fund	8.3	4.5
Special Development Fund (Caribbean Development Bank)	17.0	17.4
For reference:		
Canada's GNP as a share in total DAC	3.0	2.6

1. As of June 1997.
Source: OECD.

Together with "like-minded" countries, Canada has also played a lead role in encouraging the multilateral development banks to shift their priority from infrastructure investment towards social sector investment and sustainable development.

At the World Bank, Canada has been promoting poverty reduction as the key priority; it has encouraged a co-ordinated World Bank Group approach to private sector development; continued to press the Bank to become more active in promoting good governance; and advocated a better integration of environmental considerations into the Bank's operations. CIDA has also been very active in advocating increased attention to the gender aspects of economic reform, notably in the context of the Special Programme of Assistance for Africa. The multi-donor group on Structural Adjustment and Gender in Africa (SAGA), in which CIDA has played a leading role, has proven to be an excellent model for policy dialogue at many levels.

Canada has been pursuing the same objectives on the Boards of all the regional development banks of which it is a member. Recent achievements in this regard include the adoption of governance as an allocation criteria for lending by the African Development Bank; the establishment by the Asian Development Bank of a new policy on energy and forestry, which takes environmental policies fully into account; and the initiation of a discussion regarding excessive military expenditures in the Inter-American Development Bank.

Canada also pays great attention to the financial integrity of these organisations. In 1994-95, CIDA carried out a comprehensive financial viability study of each of the regional development banks and is now actively pursuing implementation of the study's recommendations.

Since 1995, an annual report has been submitted to Parliament on Canada's involvement in the regional development banks. The *Report to Parliament – Canada's Participation during 1995 in the Regional Development Banks* – describes the importance of the regional development banks for Canada and Canada's financial participation, including technical co-operation funds. It includes an assessment of the activities of these banks in terms of Canada's six programme priorities and their managerial efficiency and Canadian procurement from these banks.

Canada places emphasis on improving the co-ordination and effectiveness of multilateral organisations, notably those involved in humanitarian assistance and was at the forefront in helping establish the UN Department of Humanitarian Affairs, with the aim of contributing to better co-ordination of emergency assistance in the field. Canada has also been working with other donor countries to promote UN system reform, including of the Security Council, the Economic and Social Council and individual bodies such as the UNDP, the World Health Organisation (WHO) and the UN Secretariat itself, notably in connection with its management of peacekeeping functions. Canada contributed substantially to discussions on the Secretary-General's *Agenda for Development*, which outlines the UN's potential role in promoting social and economic development.

As in most DAC Member countries, there is less direct involvement and support in Canada for multilateral assistance relative to assistance provided on a bilateral basis or through the voluntary sector. In contrast to the sharp reactions to the reduction in CIDA support to voluntary sector projects as a result of ODA budget cuts, the significant reduction in Canadian participation in the Asian and African Development Funds has not elicited much reaction among the Canadian public, which tends to consider the multilateral system as unfocused, inefficient and in need of serious reform.

Canada thus faces two critical challenges with regard to its participation in the multilateral system:

- maintaining Canada's influence and credibility despite significant reductions in Canada's financial support; and

- increasing the Canadian public's understanding of the critical role played by the multilateral system in pursuing Canada's foreign policy and development objectives.

The Commonwealth and the Francophonie

Canada is the only donor in both the Commonwealth and the Francophonie. Following the 1995 foreign policy review, the policy of allocating 65 per cent of bilateral assistance to developing countries in these two groups has been discontinued. Over the past few years, Canada has played an active role in placing the issues of good governance and conflict prevention on the agenda of these two organisations.

CIDA contributes to the Special Development Programme (*Programme spécial de développement*) of the *Agence de coopération culturelle et technique* and has been providing financial support to the Francophonie Television network, TV5, through Heritage Canada.

Together with other Commonwealth donors, Canada agreed at the 1997 Edinburgh Heads of Government meeting to fund an international trade and access facility to provide technical advice on adjusting to and taking advantage of the opportunities of globalisation. The facility will be administered under the Commonwealth Fund for Technical Co-operation.

3

CIDA: AN ORGANISATION IN RENEWAL

A. TOWARDS A RESULTS-BASED CULTURE AND MANAGEMENT SYSTEM

1. Reports by the Auditor-General

The Office of the Auditor-General of Canada conducts independent audits and examinations that provide objective information and advice to Parliament. One of the Auditor-General's responsibilities is to assess whether government programmes are being run economically and efficiently, and whether the government has the means to measure the effectiveness of its programmes. In recent years, the Auditor-General has carried out three such "value-for-money" or "performance" audits of monies spent from the International Assistance Envelope. These audits focused on regional development banks (Auditor-General's 1992 Report), management of bilateral programmes (1993 Report) and technical assistance contributions to Central and Eastern Europe (1994 Report).

An open and collaborative partnership has developed between CIDA and the Office of the Auditor-General that is not often found between DAC donor agencies and government auditors. In Canada, the Auditor-General has not only identified areas of concern, but is also collaborating with CIDA and monitoring its efforts to address those concerns.

CIDA's management of bilateral economic and social development programmes

In 1993, the Auditor-General presented to Parliament the results of a value-for-money audit of CIDA's management of its bilateral programmes. The audit was conducted with a view to:

- providing objective information, advice and assurance to help Parliament scrutinise CIDA's use of its resources and management for results;
- promoting accountability and good practices by CIDA in managing for results; and
- highlighting areas for improving CIDA's management of its country programmes and projects.

The Auditor-General found that there was considerable scope to improve CIDA's performance. In particular, there was a need to improve accountability and strengthen management effectiveness. An analysis of a sample of bilateral programmes and projects showed that in the majority of cases the potential for sustainable benefits could be questioned. The main points from the 1993 audit are presented in Box 6.

The Auditor-General's examination of CIDA coincided with an internal Strategic Management Review which identified some similar lessons for the Agency. The CIDA executive was determined to address these shared concerns and, in response, CIDA made a commitment to Parliament to take actions on several fronts aimed at transforming the Agency into a more results-oriented, focused, efficient and accountable organisation. A Renewal Plan was launched in 1994, incorporating actions necessary to address the Auditor-General's concerns.

An important element of the work of the Office of the Auditor-General is its follow-up on actions taken in response to the concerns raised in its reports to Parliament. In the case of the 1993 audit, CIDA and the Office of the Auditor-General agreed to adopt a new approach, a "phased follow-up", to monitor implementation of CIDA's Renewal Plan. The follow-up has three phases, each consisting of two parts:

- *Phase* I – to assess whether CIDA is addressing the Auditor-General's principal concerns, comprising:
  - a self-assessment prepared by CIDA of actions taken (completed in July 1995) with comments and reactions from the Auditor-General;
  - the development of a Bilateral Project Performance Review System;

Box 6. **Main Points in the Auditor-General's 1993 Report**

- "Official Development Assistance is a significant aspect of Canada's foreign policy. For 25 years CIDA has been the main conduit for delivering development assistance. Annual expenditures for bilateral economic and social development assistance exceed one billion dollars.

- We conducted this audit taking into account the increasing international awareness that continued investment in development projects that are not likely to be sustained beyond donors' financial assistance represents a questionable use of scarce resources.

- In its ability to meet development needs of the nineties, the Agency has been losing ground. Current performance has not maximised the use of resources and has not led sufficiently to self-reliant development. There is considerable scope to improve CIDA's performance in promoting enduring benefits from its investments.

- CIDA's bilateral programs need to concentrate more on those countries and activities where there is the greatest potential.

- Lessons learned from 25 years' experience show a need to resolve conflicts among multiple objectives and to establish a more results-oriented, focused, businesslike and accountable style of operation. They also call for dedication to the basic objectives, such as fighting poverty and helping people help themselves, that Canada has affirmed repeatedly over many years.

- None of these changes will be easy to make, since they will require a change in mindset, skills and culture, and strong ministerial support. Their successful implementation will depend on the will to reform, not only among management and staff of the Agency but also among those who act as its development partners, in Canada and in the developing countries where CIDA operates."

Source: *Report of the Auditor General of Canada to the House of Commons*, November 1996, Exhibit 29.2.

- *Phase* II – to assess the progress of CIDA's renewal at field level, comprising:
  - an examination of CIDA-led pilot projects illustrating the application of its performance review system in the field; and
  - a self-assessment prepared by CIDA of Phase II results (completed in July 1996), with comments and reactions from the Auditor-General; and
- *Phase* III – to assess the quality of CIDA's programmes and projects and the reporting thereon, comprising:
  - an audit by the Auditor-General of selected country programmes and projects, focusing on the measurement of results; and
  - the Auditor-General's opinion on the extent to which CIDA's actions have satisfactorily resolved concerns raised in its 1993 Report.

The phased follow-up approach is intended to foster greater ownership of the Auditor-General's concerns by CIDA, increase commitment to addressing those concerns and build a constructive working

relationship between the two organisations. For its part, the Office of the Auditor-General has been actively involved with CIDA to address the Auditor-General's recommendations.

Follow-up: Phase I

In July 1995, CIDA provided the Auditor-General with its self-assessment of progress during Phase I of the follow-up. CIDA's assessment was that progress had been significant and key improvements had been made in a number of areas. Reforms had initially focused on management practices in order to improve CIDA's ability to report on achievements in implementing the *Canada in the World* objectives. CIDA's reforms included:

- the introduction of a corporate planning process to translate policy objectives and priorities into plans, expected results and performance indicators;
- enhanced co-ordination and collaboration with DFAIT;
- improved cost-effectiveness through streamlining of the organisational structure, the planning and approval process for geographic

projects, the contracting regime and personnel and administrative processes;

- the implementation of the new *Policy for Performance Review* to improve assessment and
reporting on aid effectiveness; and

- improvement in management and reporting
capacity through the installation of information and technology infrastructure to support
CIDA's business objectives.

Work towards elaborating the *Policy on Results-
based Management* contributed towards enhancing
awareness in CIDA of the importance of managing
for results as a means of achieving and demonstrat-
ing aid results.

Commenting on CIDA's self-assessment, the
Office of the Auditor-General found that the principal concerns in its 1993 audit were being addressed
at CIDA headquarters. But the next steps were more
crucial – the effective implementation of the new
policies and practices, particularly in the field. The
main points from the Auditor-General's report on
actions during Phase I are presented in Box 7.

Follow-up: Phase II

In July 1996, CIDA informed the Auditor-General
of further accomplishments in its renewal process:

- CIDA had introduced a *Policy on Results-based
Management* and was implementing it. The
Agency was launching a results-based management training and skills development
programme;

- CIDA was putting in place a performance
measurement system that would encompass
project design, monitoring, completion
reporting, evaluation and audit;

- CIDA had developed, tested and commenced implementing the *Framework of Results
and Key Success Factors* – the core of the Bilateral Project Performance Review System – to
assess the performance of its bilateral
projects; and

- CIDA had started to plan a performance
database and to work on indicators.

CIDA highlighted the fact that these achievements had taken place during a difficult time for the

---

Box 7.   **Main Points in the Auditor-General's 1995 Report**

- "CIDA's self-assessment report addresses the principal concerns raised in our Report. The Agency has
developed a results-based management concept to strengthen its effectiveness. The clarity with which
CIDA has acknowledged its accountability to Parliament for results and the emphasis it is placing on
coherence in pursuing the government's priorities in Official Development Assistance are noteworthy.
- Insightful analysis of Canada's strengths and how they correspond with developing countries' needs, as
well as courageous decisions, will continue to be required to achieve the policy objectives set by the
government.
- The need remains for developing a contracting approach that defines the respective accountabilities and
risks of both CIDA and its executing agents in the new context of results-based management.
- There is also a call for greater transparency. Canadians want to be sure that their aid dollars are being
used effectively – that their help is making a difference in the lives of people benefiting from Canadian
assistance by increasing their self-reliance.
- It would therefore be timely to accelerate the development of indicators that are simple and usable for
measuring and reporting on the Agency's results. Any further delay in this area could well adversely
impact on CIDA's credibility. CIDA needs a comprehensive tracking and reporting system to assess the
quality and status of its projects.
- The report on Phase II of the "phased follow-up", due in 1996, will focus on how successfully CIDA has
commenced implementing its results-based management concept in the field.
- In a time of substantial budget cutbacks, it is more important than ever that CIDA be in a position to
demonstrate to Parliament which of its channels and programme instruments are yielding the best results
in achieving those objectives that have the highest priority."

Source: Report of the Auditor General of Canada to the House of Commons, November 1996, Exhibit 29.5.

international development community. Development assistance was being provided in an increasingly volatile and uncertain environment and aid budgets were decreasing. Donors' activities had expanded to include new countries and complex areas of social development, such as democratic development and human rights. There is no consensus on how to measure outcomes and longer-term impacts in these complex areas and attributing results to particular donor actions is difficult. CIDA believed the improvements it had made and planned to introduce would enhance the Agency's ability to learn from experience, improve decision making and better report on results.

Examining CIDA's Phase II self-assessment, the Auditor-General expressed satisfaction that one of the Agency's major initiatives – the *Framework of Results for Key Success Factors* – was beginning to respond to the need for CIDA to strengthen its procedures for measuring and reporting on its programme effectiveness. While acknowledging the difficult challenges faced by CIDA in fulfilling its mandate, the Auditor-General emphasized the

Agency's responsibility for "setting achievable objectives, achieving results and reporting thereon". In the Auditor-General's view, "the emphasis now needs to be on implementing this approach and on meeting related reporting requirements". The Auditor-General's comments on CIDA's reported actions during Phase II of the follow-up are presented in Box 8.

Follow-up: Phase III

As part of Phase III of the follow-up, the Auditor-General is now conducting an audit to formulate an opinion on the extent to which CIDA's actions have satisfactorily resolved the main concerns raised in its 1993 Report. In addition, this audit will assess the quality of CIDA's programmes and projects, and the reporting on these. The three-phased follow-up approach is seen to have had several advantages. In particular, it has given CIDA time to implement major reforms, always a challenging task in a large, complex, international organisation. It is important to note that the Auditor-General's role during the first two phases has been limited to reviewing

---

Box 8. **Main Points in the Auditor-General's November 1996 Report**

"CIDA has introduced a Policy on Results-Based Management and is implementing it. The Agency has since developed a Framework of Results and Key Success Factors for measuring its results at the project level. It has also identified a set of Assessment Tools to enable the Framework to be used by operating personnel. These are the first of several steps required to build an effective performance measurement system. They begin to respond to our concern that the Agency did not have satisfactory procedures to measure and report on its effectiveness.

CIDA needs to move ahead with courage and determination if it is to realise practical benefits from the new concepts and policies it has devised. At this time, there is a need to:

- clarify how pursuing objectives at the project level contributes toward achieving objectives at the country program level and, as appropriate, the higher-level objectives specified by the government in *Canada in the World*;

- emphasize the application of the Framework and Assessment Tools for ongoing monitoring of results during the implementation stages of programs and projects;

- further improve reporting on performance; and

- develop a practical and realistic workplan with a timetable for implementing the system.

The challenge for the Agency is indeed significant. First, the Bilateral Project Performance Review System for measuring and reporting on results is still in an early stage of development. The System needs to be further developed in consultation with Canadian executing agents and host country institutions and then tested for its suitability by operating personnel in the field. This will take time to implement, given that work on critical aspects, such as the linkage between the information that will be provided by the System and the information reported to Parliament, is not sufficiently advanced. Second, all the key tools needed for strengthening the Agency's management effectiveness and accountability have not yet been fully developed."

Source: *Report of the Auditor General of Canada to the House of Commons*, November 1996, paragraphs 29.7 to 29.9.

CIDA's self-assessments. Based on the findings of its Phase III audit, the Auditor-General will present an assessment of CIDA's progress in a Report to Parliament in late 1998.

The Office of the Auditor-General has already noted a shift in attitudes and approaches over the period of its collaboration with CIDA and has witnessed changes in the mindset of CIDA staff, leading CIDA to become more results oriented. While it is still difficult for the Auditor-General to determine whether the Agency is achieving better results, progress has been noted as regards the self-sustainability of bilateral projects. The Auditor-General continues to encourage CIDA to involve beneficiaries more in its evaluations and to make a stronger link between the achievement of results and budget allocations.

2. Performance review, results-based management and the Framework of Results and Key Success Factors

CIDA has introduced several management reforms to transform the Agency into a more results-oriented and accountable organisation, and in so doing address the concerns raised in the 1993 Auditor-General's Report. The principal management initiatives are presented here.

Policy for Performance Review

In July 1994, CIDA introduced a *Policy for Performance Review* to allow the Agency to assess effectiveness with respect to development and operational results. This policy established a new framework for the audit and evaluation functions and has had the effect of creating a closer connection between the Performance Review Branch and operational branches at CIDA. The purpose of the new policy is to ensure that CIDA managers and staff have credible, timely and useful information on the performance of the Agency's policies, programmes, projects, operations and other activities, including the development results they achieve. Implementing the policy requires the identification of intended development and operational results and the establishment of appropriate indicators to measure effectiveness. The policy operates at three levels: continuous performance measurement (as a branch function); evaluation and internal audit (as corporate functions); and a combination of these with other sources of information and analysis to support external reporting on CIDA activities.

Results-based management

CIDA formally adopted results-based management as its main management tool in May 1996. CIDA's *Policy on Results-Based Management* states that:

"Results-based management is integral to the Agency's management philosophy and practice. CIDA will systematically focus on results to ensure that it employs management practices which optimise value for money and the prudent use of its human and financial resources. CIDA will report on its results in order to inform Parliament and Canadians of its development achievements."

The progressive implementation of results-based management is expected to assist CIDA in its efforts towards continuous improvement in results-orientation, focus, efficiency and accountability. It is playing an important role in the Agency's continuing development as a learning organisation, by focusing attention on results from the formulation of country/regional programme frameworks to *ex post* evaluation. It embraces six principles: simplicity; learning by doing; broad application; partnership; accountability and transparency. CIDA staff are finding results-based management approaches to be useful for handling the risks inherent in many development co-operation actions and for clarifying respective responsibilities with partners. A note on results-based management is given in Box 9.

Framework of Results and Key Success Factors

The *Framework of Results and Key Success Factors* is the core of the Bilateral Project Performance Review System. The Framework is designed to generate a consistent body of information on each project that can also be synthesised or aggregated to provide an indication of performance at the programme, branch and agency levels. The information produced should enable staff to manage better for results, learn from experience and report on achievements. The Framework is not only an *ex post* tool, but also aims to assist in the assessment of both project-specific and general factors on an on-going basis throughout the project cycle, facilitating the early identification of necessary corrective actions, ranging from design modification to project reformulation.

The Framework defines the factors to be considered in assessing aid effectiveness and so

Box 9. **Results-Based Management**
A *note by the New Zealand Examiner*

Like other donor agencies, CIDA continues to look for ways to enhance the efficiency, effectiveness and impact of its development co-operation efforts. And the public and Parliaments of the developed countries expect to see positive results. This raises the question of performance measurement. It has always been easier to describe and measure inputs and outputs compared to outcomes and impacts and the budget-driven imperatives of donors has reinforced a focus on inputs. However, many Programme and project evaluations have concluded that the failure to think in terms of long-term effectiveness, impacts and sustainability has meant results have often been disappointing. Also, as development agendas have placed more emphasis on issues such as capacity building, institutional strengthening, democratic development, human rights and peacebuilding, performance measurement has become more complex.

CIDA has been aware of these issues and sought to improve its performance and ability to report on results. Since the 1994 DAC Review of Canada, CIDA has taken a number of significant steps to develop and refine its management systems aimed at transforming the Agency into a results-oriented and learning organisation. There is, however, much to be done, and a number of challenges in making such a system work:

- the need to change the corporate culture to be more results-oriented, and develop appropriate self-assessment mechanisms and accountabilities for staff at all levels;
- the need to develop tools which will assist staff to be more performance-oriented (*e.g.* a revised logical framework analysis, better indicators, etc.);
- the need to build into performance measurement systems cross-cutting issues such as gender, environment and capacity building;
- the need to tailor the performance management system to the different types of assistance programmes CIDA implements;
- the need to incorporate participatory approaches and involvement of both Canadian partners and developing country partners;
- the needs to link project level performance factors to corporate goals, objectives and programme priorities; and
- the need to develop a robust information system which will enable data to be aggregated and used for performance reporting.

The Review team found that CIDA is aware of these challenges and substantial progress is being made to address these. There appears to be an acceptance of and enthusiasm for a results-oriented approach throughout the Agency as well as an effort to review progress at regular intervals against better defined indicators. A substantial training programme is being implemented to increase awareness and skills in identifying expected results, using indicators, collecting information and reporting. Managers in all of CIDA's delivery modes (*e.g.* Multilateral and Canadian Partnership) are looking at what a results-oriented approach would mean for them and developing a performance measurement framework for their work.

The new system should enable a more coherent and consistent measurement of results across the Agency with more complementarity between the analysis undertaken within operational branches and by the corporate Performance Review Branch. The Performance Review Branch is playing an important support role in promoting results-based management (*e.g.* in developing systems, tools and support mechanisms for branches) and is now working closely with branch management and staff through formal and informal networks to meet the day-to-day needs of programme managers.

It will of course be important that the focus on results-based management does not become a mechanistic management tool which itself over-simplifies the development process in the search for short-term and visible results. The focus must remain on doing development, not reporting on it. Analysis by CIDA's own Policy Branch of the relationship between results-based management and effective development in areas such as institutional and capacity development, human rights and good governance, and WID and gender equality have highlighted potential dilemmas. Programme and project design will remain a complex process, involving the interplay of political, economic, social and environmental factors. Results-based management provides a framework within which the various stakeholders can plan, implement, evaluate and report on projects. How they do so, however, will necessarily have to take into account the particular context; it must involve co-operation to define outcomes and results, flexibility to change (as experience determines this is required because of circumstances on the ground) and a willingness to learn and adapt. Results-based management should not be a return to the "blueprint" approach to project development, but be an interactive, learning and adaptive process.

(*continued on next page*)

(continued)

The essence of effective results-based management in a development agency like CIDA will be the active involvement of stakeholders in project design (*i.e.* recipient authorities, target populations, Canadian partners), agreement on relevant indicators against which to measure progress and close monitoring of results. Only in this way will ownership and sustainability be encouraged and performance improved – the essential point of results-based management. The ability to report on results will be a secondary but no less important by-product of such an approach being consistently applied throughout the Agency.

One of the principles of CIDA's results-based management policy is simplicity. It will be important that systems and procedures remain practical and useful to programme managers yet be able to provide management information for reporting purposes. The development of an effective Agency Information System will be crucial to achieving the benefits of results-based management and the ability to report results at the project, institutional, programme and corporate levels.

complements the *Policy for Performance Review*. It contains three sections:

- achievement of results – at output, outcome and impact levels;

- development factors – relevance, appropriateness, cost-effectiveness and sustainability; and

- management factors – partnership, innovation and creativity, appropriate human resource utilisation, prudence and probity, and informed and timely actions.

The Framework was first applied to bilateral projects and has now been adapted and expanded to cover the activities of the Multilateral and Canadian Partnership Branches.

B. PERFORMANCE MONITORING

Assessment of results is done at all levels of all CIDA Branches, using the *Policy on Results-Based Management* and the *Framework of Results and Key Success Factors* as the basis for a more structured approach to undertaking and reporting on evaluations. Using lessons learnt while implementing the *Policy for Performance Review* and the experience of working in a results-based management context, the performance review policy was updated in November 1996 to clarify the respective roles of the corporate Performance Review Branch and other CIDA Branches. The Performance Review Branch is responsible for corporate review, including audits, evaluations and performance reviews of programme priorities. Branch Vice-Presidents and their line managers are responsible for performance measurement – programme, project and institutional monitoring, end-

of-project reporting, institutional assessment and special studies (see also Box 9).

The Performance Review Branch has reported directly to the President of CIDA since 1 October 1997. It is headed by a Director-General, supported by a Director for Evaluation, a Director for Internal Audit and a Director for Results-based Management, 11 professionals and four support staff. The Branch's budget for 1997-98 is C$ 4.3 million, 0.3 per cent of CIDA's total budget. Each programme branch has a Performance Review Officer.

The Performance Review Branch is mandated to review and report on the performance of CIDA's six programme priorities. Each priority is the subject of a performance review, following which a synthesis report is produced drawing together the most significant findings and recommending improvements and future directions. After approval by the CIDA executive, these synthesis reports are available for general distribution. A performance review of WID/Gender Equity was completed in 1996, although the management response and communication approach for releasing the synthesis report are still under consideration. A review of Basic Human Needs was undertaken in 1997 and a review of Infrastructure Services is planned for 1998. Performance reviews of Private Sector Development; Environment; and Human Rights, Democracy and Good Governance will be conducted from 1999 to 2001. A performance review of Food Aid was also completed in 1997. As regards CIDA's overarching poverty reduction policy, a one-year retrospective was produced in October 1996 (see Chapter 2, Section B).

All CIDA evaluation reports and Branch reports are available to the public on request. Evaluations are also available on CD-ROM and via Internet. CIDA prepares an annual report on plans and priorities for Parliament, known as Part III of the Estimates. As from 1997, CIDA has complemented the information available on both expected and actual results by providing Parliament with an annual performance report.

Compared to many other DAC donors, CIDA's evaluation function is well developed. The DAC's *Principles for the Evaluation of Development Assistance* set out six points of general guidance on the role of aid evaluation in the aid management process. CIDA is broadly in conformity with these recommendations as regards evaluation policy, role and responsibilities; impartiality and independence; openness and availability of results; application and feedback of results; and integration of evaluation in the planning process. One weak point concerns the participation of recipients in the evaluation process. CIDA has not yet conducted reviews with the full participation of beneficiaries. Beneficiaries do however participate where possible in on-going assessments and CIDA has conducted training programmes for recipients and their governments.

C. HUMAN RESOURCE RENEWAL

In the context of a federal programme to revitalise the public sector work force, "La Relève", and its own Corporate Renewal Plan, CIDA has been implementing a number of initiatives to develop its human resource base in line with its new programme priorities and the shift in focus from physical infrastructure to softer sectors. This had, in particular, to address the reality of a rapidly ageing workforce: about half the CIDA staff in senior positions will be eligible for retirement within ten years. Key initiatives in this area include an early retirement programme, the recruitment of staff at entry, intermediate and senior levels, a regular cycle of promotion, based on competitions, and a heavy

emphasis on training at all levels, in line with the requirements of CIDA's rapidly changing programme portfolio.

Although these changes took place during a period when CIDA was reducing the size of its workforce as a result of budget reductions, staff morale has remained high. This is attributable both to sensitive and skilful handling of the situation by CIDA management and to the professional commitment of outgoing CIDA staff, who understood the critical importance of the renewal initiative for CIDA's future ability to fulfil its mandate.

D. RECENTRALISATION AND PROJECT SUPPORT UNITS

In the late 1980s, CIDA moved to a decentralised aid management system, through significant deployment of staff to country-specific or regional offices overseas. This policy was reversed in 1993, largely due to cost considerations, and CIDA has now reverted to its former system whereby CIDA projects are managed largely from headquarters. A small number of CIDA staff (about 8 per cent of total staff strength, see Table 4) are posted to High Commissions and embassies to provide assistance with programme identification and implementation, notably in countries with significant aid programmes. The management of the local Canada Fund is normally entrusted to Ambassadors or High Commissioners.

Following the recentralisation of its staff, CIDA has developed innovative means of maintaining close relationships with partner countries and organisations, exploiting all the possibilities afforded by new communication technology, making maximum use of locally-available expertise and despatching senior Canadian experts in support of specific projects. This approach is well illustrated by the case of South Africa (see Box 1). It can be very

Table 4. **CIDA staffing levels**

	31 March 1993	31 March 1994	31 March 1995	31 March 1996	31 March 1997
Headquarters	1 078	1 068	1 054	1 033	1 058
Abroad	161	122	107	106	101
On leave	107	125	112	86	101
Seconded	16	21	25	17	26
Total	**1 362**	**1 336**	**1 298**	**1 242**	**1 286**

Source: CIDA.

effective in connection with specialised projects, notably in some kinds of governance projects or where the necessary expertise is not readily available locally. At the same time, this approach can have limitations, as identified in a review of CIDA's programming experience in the area of human rights and governance, completed in 1994, which found that CIDA's work had been most effective when there had been a strong field presence to support programming.

While not directly addressing this issue, CIDA is increasing its reliance on local "Project (or Programme) Support Units" to provide technical, clerical and logistical support to projects and maintain regular liaison with local partners. Composed essentially of locally-hired staff, these Units are occasionally headed by CIDA staff on temporary leave from the Agency, which also provides CIDA with an additional means for its staff to gain field exposure. The operation of Project Support Units is scheduled to be reviewed and evaluated in 1998.

Over the past few years, CIDA has shifted from one tactic to the other as regards personnel presence at field level. The decision to recentralise was based on cost considerations rather than a considered assessment of the relative advantages of centralised and decentralised models. If such an assessment were conducted today, recent administrative reforms, most notably the streamlined contracting system, might argue in favour of a shift towards increased decentralisation. Although the current system may be appropriate in CIDA's current budget environment, it is likely to show definite limitations in the event of a significant expansion in programming. CIDA could explore the scope for a more diversified approach to this question, and consider a greater degree of decentralisation when programme contents and conditions in the partner country warrant it (it appears that there is, *de facto*, a certain degree of flexibility along these lines, *cf.* the case of China).

E. MAINSTREAMING OF SECTORAL EXPERTISE

The decision to redeploy sector specialists, previously grouped in operational "Technical Advisory Units" to operational functions including programme management, represented an important shift in support of objective-based programming. This aimed to break away from a traditional sector focus and to harness the considerable expertise of CIDA's sectoral specialists, in areas ranging from infrastructure to environment, in direct support of CIDA's development objectives.

The drawback, in the form of a dilution of available technical expertise, remains an unresolved issue. The introduction of "standing offer" arrangements (see Section G below) contributes to alleviating this constraint by providing a quick and cost-effective means of recruiting necessary technical expertise when required. However, the availability of in-house expertise remains essential in order to assess the technical qualifications of contracted experts. Systems of networking among technical experts, facilitated by improvements in communications technology is a response to this. However, as in other aid agencies which are adopting similar approaches, the ultimate question is whether mainstreaming or concentration proves to be the most effective way of harnessing professional expertise.

These issues, which are of critical relevance to CIDA's focus on project quality, will require careful monitoring in the future.

F. INFORMATION SYSTEMS

A critical requirement for the full-scale implementation of CIDA's results-based management approach is the development of an integrated information system allowing the recording and retrieval of key information regarding all aspects of on-going programme management. At present, however, critical financial accounting, project management and other qualitative information regarding the implementation status and performance of projects is not readily available in a usable form. Budget constraints and accountability requirements make it all the more urgent to develop such a system.

Information management renewal has been identified by CIDA management as a major challenge over the next few years, requiring considerable investment in financial and human resources. In the short term, CIDA has devoted significant human resources to planning its new information system. The direct cost is estimated at around C$ 50 million.

CIDA expects that this significant information management and technology renewal project will result in improved access to *a*) more and better Agency information (on projects, programmes, results, financial and human resources and contracts), *b*) specialised knowledge, and *c*) improved communications with partners and colleagues in the world.

CIDA's information renewal will be implemented in the context of the Government of Canada's Financial Information Strategy, which requires all agencies of the government to comply with new financial reporting standards and specifications by 2000.

G. PROCUREMENT OF SERVICES: NEW CONTRACTING SYSTEM

Following a wide consultation process with Canadian private- and voluntary-sector partners, CIDA has streamlined its contracting system with a view to increasing the transparency, speed and efficiency of transactions. Principal features of the new system, which is being implemented on a pilot basis over the period January 1997 to March 1998, include:

- A single set of procedures for not-for-profit and private-sector contacts. This allows these two types of organisations to bid on bilateral contracts, or to submit project proposals for consideration by CIDA's bilateral branches. In addition to providing equal treatment for all interested CIDA partners, this system allows voluntary organisations and private sector firms to combine their distinct strengths and resources and submit bids or project proposals jointly. With respect to the supply of goods, competition will remain limited to the private sector.

- A one-step contracting procedure, which dispenses with the pre-qualification stage previously required. This allows CIDA to select the "best value" proposal received (technical merit and cost), based on a financial and technical bid. CIDA procurement is subject to an independent bid dispute mechanism.

"Standing Offer Arrangements" represent another important innovation for CIDA. This system, whereby a firm or individual consultant is recruited on a "standby basis" to provide services as, if and when needed, allows CIDA ready access to specific technical resources not available in-house. Standing offers, which are normally made for a three-year period, are announced on an electronic tendering service as well as on CIDA's Internet site.

Within the Canadian Partnership Branch, WID and Gender Equity Guidelines were revised to require that Canadian private sector firms planning to make a submission to CIDA INC undertake a gender analysis at the feasibility-study stage and develop an appropriate gender equity strategy based on the findings. The objectives of these guidelines are to make gender analysis integral to every project and to expected results.

H. TECHNICAL CO-OPERATION AND CAPACITY DEVELOPMENT

As a result of a steady decline in large infrastructure projects, more and more CIDA programming has effectively taken on a "technical co-operation" nature, focusing on human resource and institutional development.

Along with many other DAC donors, CIDA is increasingly moving from traditional technical co-operation towards the concept of capacity development, whereby developing country partners take the lead in project design and implementation. This poses a special challenge for CIDA in the context of its results-based management approach. A critical issue in this regard is reconciling the need to ensure that projects are truly owned by developing country partners and managed according to their own priorities, yet comply with CIDA's own rigorous accountability requirements. Balancing these potentially contradictory considerations requires the results-based management process itself to be owned by partners. Important challenges ahead thus include the development of performance indicators and monitoring techniques which themselves foster leadership by partners and directly contribute to project objectives. An internal network on capacity building/technical co-operation operates within CIDA to promote collective thinking and sharing of concepts. CIDA plays a leading role in the Informal DAC Network on Technical Co-operation.

4

PARTNERSHIPS IN CANADIAN DEVELOPMENT CO-OPERATION: POLICIES AND PRACTICES

The Government of Canada recognises that civil society partners, including grassroots organisations, development and environmental organisations, churches, labour unions, professional associations and co-operatives, are a key source of the skills, know-how and technology needed to fulfil the mandate of the ODA programme. The extent and scope of collaboration between CIDA and voluntary sector organisations in Canada and developing countries remains a defining feature of Canada's aid programme. During a field visit to South Africa in preparation for this review, the Secretariat was able to appreciate the extent to which civil society partners are important for Canada's programme (see Box 10 which describes some examples of programming initiatives being carried out with Canadian civil society partners). The Canadian voluntary sector also plays an essential role in mobilising the Canadian public in support of international development. In 1996-97, CIDA direct support to the voluntary (not-for-profit) sector accounted for 9.1 per cent of total ODA. This figure does not include support from the geographic branches.

The last DAC Review of Canada in 1994 pointed to the great number and variety of instruments through which CIDA collaborated with non-governmental partners. This had led to administrative and managerial difficulties and a perceived lack of focus. This situation has now been rectified through a thorough re-organisation of CIDA's partnership with civil society actors.

A. FRAMEWORK FOR A RENEWED RELATIONSHIP

To fulfil the commitment made in *Canada in the World*, CIDA has conducted a comprehensive consultation process – involving over 500 organisations across the country – to formulate a framework to guide its relationship with civil society partners, based on the principle of complementarity. This aimed to combine CIDA's comparative advantage in the areas of institutional knowledge, technical expertise and co-ordination with the special strengths of non-governmental organisations, including in connection with the implementation of the *Government of Canada's Policy for CIDA on Human Rights, Democratisation and Good Governance*.

The *Framework for a Renewed Relationship* received Ministerial approval in October 1996. Its guiding principles include:

- **Mutual respect**. While recognising that the voluntary sector's roles and objectives are broader than those of CIDA, the specific programmes supported by CIDA are expected to contribute to fulfilling the mandate of Canada's ODA programme.

- **Accountability**. CIDA and voluntary organisations recognise that together, they are accountable to Parliament and the Canadian public for reporting on initiatives on which they collaborate.

- **Participation and dialogue**. CIDA seeks to collaborate with voluntary organisations from all parts of the country and all sectors of society and to work with organisations that effectively engage the Canadian public in Canada's international development effort.

In operational terms, the implementation of these principles involves the provision of financial support, on a cost-sharing basis, for programmes and projects conceived and implemented by Canadian voluntary organisations in close association with their developing country partners, and which fall within the mandate and priorities set for the ODA programme ("responsive programming"). CIDA also draws upon the special skills and expertise of voluntary sector partners in connection with the implementation of programmes funded through the geographic branches, including in the areas of food aid and humanitarian assistance. In this connection, Canadian NGOs must face the dilemmas involved in developing genuine partnerships with their

Box 10. **CIDA in South Africa: Partnerships in the Field**

The CIDA bilateral programme is the main channel for Canadian development assistance to South Africa and addresses four priority areas: governance; human resource development; support to civil society; and economic development. Nearly 50 per cent of the programme supports human resource development and education, which the South African government has designated as a high priority area. The CIDA programme aims to assist South Africa with its immediate transition challenges in the post-apartheid era by providing South Africa with access to relevant Canadian expertise, models, best practices and lessons learnt. Projects have been developed in response to needs articulated by South Africans that conform to South Africa's own development strategies. Participatory planning and local ownership are features of both programme- and project-level activities.

The Secretariat was able to observe these essential features during a field visit to South Africa in preparation for this review. It was clear from visits to a selection of projects that the programme is appreciated by South African counterparts and that CIDA is leveraging its resources to deliver high-impact development assistance. The programme is in harmony with the goals and principles of *Shaping the 21st Century: The Contribution of Development Co-operation.*

Charter of Rights Project

The Bill of Rights, enshrined in the South African constitution, shares many similarities with the 1981 Canadian Charter of Rights and Freedoms. Canadian experience since its Charter came into force has created legal expertise and jurisprudence of great relevance and interest to the South African legal community. The Charter of Rights Project is a collaborative partnership between the Canadian Bar Association and the Legal Resource Centre (LRC) in Johannesburg, one of South Africa's leading institutions involved in constitutional litigation. The project aims to contribute to the process of constitutional development in South Africa through strengthening the capacity of the LRC's Constitutional Litigation Unit; building a co-operative network of South African constitutional lawyers with improved skills and capacity; providing skilled and sustainable litigation services on constitutional rights issues; and ensuring adequate access to relevant Canadian and other international precedents, expertise, material and resources in support of constitutional test cases. The project has a budget of C\$ 4.4 million and is scheduled to run over four years.

The Constitutional Litigation Unit now interacts on a regular basis with the Canadian Bar Association. As part of this project, each member of the Unit can train for six weeks with the Association in Canada and a two-way residency programme has been established for selected staff to spend three months with the other institution. These interchanges have formed the basis for networking opportunities useful for staff of the Unit. The networks established and the personal contacts made should continue after the project's completion. The Unit can also benefit from advice from Canadian lawyers when preparing cases, for example through telephone conferences. The Constitutional Litigation Unit considers the capacity development and access to expert advice they receive from the Canadian Bar Association are far more useful than simply receiving a cash grant. This project is an example of CIDA supporting activities where Canada has a clear comparative advantage.

Local Elections Support Project

As part of the run-up to the first local government elections scheduled for 1 November 1995, an election information centre, known as "LOGIC": the Local Government Information Centre, was established by the Institute for Democracy in South Africa (IDASA). IDASA was created in 1986 by two ex-ministers who found there was a need for an institute focusing on democracy which would stimulate debate and provide forums for discussion. In 1992, the Institute redefined its role as "assisting the success of negotiations and the transition to a non-racial democracy" and began to focus its work on issues which were defined as "potential obstacles to the transition process"; mainly in the areas of local government, education, security and economics.

CIDA's Local Elections Support Project provided C\$ 1.6 million of funding for the Local Government Information Centre. The Project was managed by a local steering committee which included representatives from the Ministries of Provincial Affairs and Constitutional Development. The Centre provided a full range of election-related information to the public, including via a 1-800 free telephone service which received over 270 000 calls from both voters and election administrators. The Centre was considered highly successful and is now being promoted as a transferable mechanism for other elections.

(continued on next page)

(continued)

IDASA is working with CIDA on other projects (*e.g.* the Migration Policy Project) and with other donors. IDASA rates CIDA highly as a partner. It finds CIDA's reporting requirements to be reasonable and appreciates that CIDA is clear about its own agenda. CIDA provides helpful advice but also gives IDASA enough freedom to get on with implementing projects.

Civil Society Capacity Development Project

Following the 1994 multi-racial elections in South Africa, most donors moved from channelling their aid through NGOs to a government-to-government approach. Consequently, some NGOs faced a funding crisis in the post-election period. Concerned about deteriorating civil society capacity and possible difficulties for NGOs to continue delivering services to the poor, CIDA asked Canadian civil society organisations to identify key South African NGOs which would benefit from support in the form of capacity development. Eleven sub-projects were developed as part of this initiative scheduled to run for three years with a budget of C$ 3.2 million.

One sub-project (with a budget of C$ 500 000) concerned the NGO "Get Ahead". Get Ahead initially had activities in four areas: micro finance; training; health; and social services development. Through a Canadian NGO, Get Ahead received support in a number of forms, including training and assistance in clarifying Get Ahead's business lines and in selecting an appropriate legal structure for its activities. This resulted in the organisation being split into a registered company, *Get Ahead Financial Services*, to handle the micro-credit business and the *Get Ahead Foundation*, to support the remaining three activities. Subsequently, *Get Ahead Financial Services* received training from Canadians in micro-credit operations, however, it was felt that the course offered was not well adapted to the South African context and that it would have been more beneficial to fund this training through a South African organisation.

While in South Africa, the Secretariat visited a selection of *Get Ahead Financial Services* micro-credit clients in Mamelodi, near Pretoria. A small hardware business is now able to provide building materials to people recently arrived in the township or improving their accommodation. A traditional medicine supplier uses her loans to pay for petrol to collect supplies, to pay trackers to find particular roots and for stock purchasing and working capital for the business. A small welding business specialising in window frames is now supplying the government and will be receiving training from the *Get Ahead Foundation* on government tendering requirements and meeting standards set by the South African Standards Board. For these clients, Get Ahead provided the access to credit which was vital for the development and current success of their businesses.

developing country counterparts, relinquishing a large degree of control over projects while retaining a high degree of accountability for their results.

Since September 1993, with the adoption of a formal policy on consultation with Canadian civil society stakeholders, CIDA has made consultations with its diverse group of civil society partners an integral part of its work. Consultations are held to discuss policy themes and Regional, Sub-Regional and Country Policy Frameworks and other issues of mutual interest. In order to ensure that consultations are truly open, CIDA's policy includes the provision of financial support to ensure the participation of essential stakeholders on the basis of demonstrable need. CIDA also facilitates the participation of Canadian and developing country voluntary organisations in key UN conferences and other important inter-governmental and non-governmen-

tal fora. The improved openness and transparency evident in CIDA is appreciated by stakeholders, although they hope for further progress still.

B. CIDA'S VOLUNTARY SECTOR AND SPECIAL PROJECTS

Following a thorough re-organisation in 1995-96, CIDA's Canadian Partnership Branch now comprises two divisions: the Institutional Co-operation Division and the NGO Division.

The Institutional Co-operation Division provides financial support for the programmes and projects initiated and managed by Canadian fund-raising NGOs, as well as institutions such as universities, colleges, co-operatives, professional associations, municipalities and unions. These projects must be based on collaboration with developing country counterparts and demonstrate a focus on results related to capacity building. International NGOs also receive support for projects focusing on the "global civil society" and addressing development issues outside the formal UN and intergovernmental systems.

The NGO Project Facility resulted in 1995 from the merger of 13 decentralised funds into one centralised instrument managed by CIDA. Endowed with a budget of C$ 14 million in 1995, it provides support to small- and medium-sized Canadian nongovernmental organisations for development co-operation activities. CIDA's contribution ranges from a minimum of C$ 25 000 up to a maximum of C$ 350 000 per year.

C. CIDA INC

CIDA's Industrial Co-operation Programme, managed by CIDA's Canadian Partnership Branch, has a mandate to harness the resources of Canada's private sector to promote sustainable development by encouraging long-term co-operation between Canada's private sector and counterparts in developing countries.

CIDA INC's objective is to promote the mutually-beneficial transfer of Canadian goods, expertise and technology and to promote investment by Canadian companies in developing countries. CIDA INC also encourages initiatives by Canadian partners to access non-Canadian sources of funding, thereby reducing their dependence on support from CIDA. This includes the provision of financial support for joint ventures to produce goods, provide services, conclude licence agreements, co-production agreements, or other types of business arrangements.

In all cases, applicants must demonstrate that project proposals will have sustainable economic, social and industrial benefits in the developing country and that the partner's company has the technical, managerial, human and financial capacities to pursue the project in a sustainable manner. Projects must also comply with the Canadian Environmental Assessment Act. Applicants must take gender issues into account in all phases of their projects and formulate a strategy to promote the participation of women in the proposed projects.

CIDA estimates that on average, every ODA dollar contributed to Canadian firms by INC, since the beginning of the programme in 1978, has generated C$ 10.88 in developing countries and C$ 5.50 in Canada. Since its inception, CIDA INC has received 10 866 project proposals, of which 6 439 (59 per cent) were approved. In 1996-97, CIDA INC accounted for 2.1 per cent of Canada's total ODA budget.

D. PROVINCIAL GOVERNMENTS

Provincial governments also play a role in Canada's development co-operation programme. Official development assistance commitments by Canadian provincial governments amounted to C$ 25 million in 1995-96 (1.0 per cent of ODA commitments in that fiscal year), C$ 22 million in 1996-97 (0.8 per cent of ODA commitments) and C$ 23 million in 1997-98 (1.0 per cent). This assistance covers a range of activities including humanitarian assistance, scholarships and support through NGOs. A number of Canadian provinces have formed twinning arrangements with South African provinces, allowing exchanges to occur to the mutual benefit of both countries (see Box 1).

5

TRADE, INVESTMENT AND AID

A. TRADE AND INVESTMENT

1. Trade relations with developing countries

Canada's trade relations are to a large extent determined by its proximity and ease of access to the world's largest economy, the United States. However, Canada is seeking to diversify its trade relations and has negotiated free-trade agreements with two developing countries – Chile and Mexico. Efforts are also being made to increase Canada's trade with fast-expanding economies in the developing world.

In 1996, Canada's exports to developing countries totalled $15.2 billion, 7.5 per cent of total Canadian exports, while the total value of imports from developing countries was $22.4 billion, the equivalent of 13.1 per cent of all imports. Developing countries in Asia accounted for 4.7 per cent of Canadian exports and 7.6 per cent of imports. In contrast, only 0.6 per cent of Canadian exports went to African countries and just under 1 per cent of imports originated in Africa.

According to the 1995 edition of the *Annual Report on the Export of Military Goods from Canada*, exports of military goods[6] to developing countries amounted to $162 million in 1995, or just over one per cent of total exports to developing countries. Saudi Arabia received military goods to a value $122 million, mostly military vehicles and related equipment and components. Thirty-eight other developing countries received military goods from Canada in 1995.

2. The North American Free-Trade Agreement (NAFTA)

More than three-quarters of Canada's trade is with the United States. Trade with the United States has grown impressively since the Canada/United States Free-Trade Agreement came into effect on 1 January 1989 and three-way trade between Canada, Mexico and the United States has been expanding at unprecedented rates since the implementation on 1 January 1994 of the North American Free-Trade Agreement (NAFTA).

The NAFTA will result in the elimination of virtually all tariffs between Canada and Mexico by 1 January 2003. Better access to the Mexican market has allowed Canadian firms to expand sales in sectors that were previously highly restricted, such as automotive products, financial services, trucking, energy and fisheries. Canadian exports have become more diversified, with value-added manufactured products accounting for more than half of total exports to Mexico in 1996. Mexico is now Canada's ninth largest export market and fourth largest source of imports. Export figures are thought to understate, perhaps by as much as 40 per cent, the real level of trade activity as many Canadian exports to Mexico transit through the United States and are frequently misidentified as regards their final destination. The main categories of imports from Mexico are machinery and equipment, automotive products and industrial goods. Canada is Mexico's third largest trading partner.

The NAFTA is creating new opportunities for Canadian exporters in high value-added niche markets. For example, Canadian producers of men's tailored suits and women's swimwear are benefitting from the greater opportunities offered through the NAFTA. In general, implementation of the NAFTA has been accompanied by advances in productivity and specialisation within the Canadian economy, greater economies of scale and improved product quality and cost competitiveness. It is, however, difficult to isolate which of these factors can be attributed in particular to Canada's expanding trading relationship with Mexico.

The Agreement has also meant dramatic increases in capital flows between Canada and Mexico. Canada was one of the most important sources of new investment in Mexico in 1996. Current investment is concentrated in mining, banking and telecommunications and potential exists for further investment in other sectors, such as gas and energy. Mexican investment in Canada remains small, but is growing.

The NAFTA was designed as an outward-looking agreement with the potential to be expanded to include new members. Negotiations aimed at Chile's accession to the NAFTA have been officially launched, but in view of a lack of Presidential fast-track authority in the United States for trade negotiations, Canada and Chile have completed negotiations on an interim bilateral free-trade agreement. The Canada/Chile Free-Trade Agreement entered into force on 5 July 1997 and provides for immediate duty-free access for 75 per cent of Canadian exports, the elimination of Chile's 11 per cent import duty on almost all remaining industrial and resource-based goods over five years and better access for a range of agricultural products.

3. Team Canada and trade diversification

Nearly 40 per cent of the Canadian economy is dependent on trade. Just 100 companies are responsible for half of Canada's exports and trade is predominantly with the United States. Such over-concentration in a key area of the economy is not considered healthy for Canada in the long run, given the importance of trade for further economic growth and employment. Consequently, efforts are being made to diversify Canada's trade relations and to position Canadian exporters better as players in the global market place. The CIDA INC programme is one channel to encourage Canadian private sector investment in developing countries and provision of services to developing country clients.

Under the name of "Team Canada", four high-level trade missions to a range of developing countries have been organised in recent years. These missions have provided participating companies and organisations with an opportunity to meet potential distributors and customers, conduct market research and, in many cases, obtain first-hand knowledge about new markets and how to break into them. The Team Canada missions have been led by the Prime Minister, accompanied by a range of people including provincial Premiers, federal ministers, mayors, representatives of educational institutions, captains of industry and young entrepreneurs. The first Team Canada mission visited China in 1994. Subsequent missions have been made to Chile (1995), India, Indonesia, Malaysia and Pakistan (1996) and South Korea, the Philippines and Thailand (1997). These missions are all considered to have been highly successful.

Canada is also working to expand trade opportunities, including for its own exporters, by supporting international efforts to promote trade liberalisation and integrate developing countries more fully into the global economy. To this end, Canada is active in fora such as APEC and the World Trade Organisation (WTO), is involved in follow-up actions to the Uruguay Round negotiations and seeks to engage multilateral institutions more fully in these efforts. CIDA does not promote trade as such, but helps in the creation of the enabling environment. Examples include CIDA support for trade policy seminars for government officials and key private-sector actors in Pakistan; support for the Vietnam/WTO training project, which aims to support Vietnam's accession to the WTO; and support to the Organisation of Eastern Caribbean States to strengthen capacity in trade policy issues, including legislative and regulatory obligations under the WTO and their implications for preparing policies on trade liberalisation.

4. Canadian investments in developing countries

The North-South Institute has made a first attempt to quantify the value of Canada's investments in developing countries.[7] The North-South Institute estimates that Canada's public and private investments (debt, equity and direct investment) in developing countries was of the order of $44 billion in 1995. The Institute estimates the annual interest, dividend and profit income from these investments was approximately $3.5 billion, which exceeds Canada's ODA to developing countries in that year ($2.1 billion).

Criticisms have been made of the methodology used to produce these estimates. The North-South Institute acknowledges that their figures do not present a complete picture of transactions between Canada and the developing world – transactions such as remittances by immigrants to developing countries and income from investments in Canada by developing countries have not been taken into account. The North-South Institute's estimation is nonetheless an interesting calculation and it is to be hoped that their methodology can be refined in the future. The point remains, however, that Canada, like many other donors, reaps tangible financial benefits from its relations with developing countries.

B. TIED AID

In 1996, two-thirds of Canadian bilateral ODA commitments[8] were tied to the procurement of goods and services in Canada, the remaining one third was untied. Canadian tied aid took the form of procurement limited to Canadian firms only (49 per cent of ODA commitments in that year), costs of maintaining refugees during their first year in Canada (11 per cent) and aid in kind, mainly food aid (8 per cent). Untied aid in the Canadian context does not necessarily mean aid contracts are open to international competitive bidding. Rather, Canada's untied aid covered local cost financing (18 per cent of commitments in 1996), debt relief (12 per cent), budget or balance-of-payment support (1 per cent) and procurement authorised in all OECD countries and substantially all aid recipient countries (1 per cent).

Canada reviewed the question of the tying of aid during its review of foreign policy in 1994. The government decided not to make any changes to its policy, which had been last revised in 1988. It has seen tied aid as important for maintaining public support, protecting the aid budget and encouraging and helping Canadian enterprises enter new markets.

Canada has a clear view of the benefits that flow back to Canadians through its aid programme and expresses this view openly. For example, CIDA's 1997-98 Part III Estimates state that:

"About 70 cents out of every Canadian development assistance dollar was used to pay for Canadian goods and services. A recent study using Statistics Canada methodology showed that in 1995-96 Canadian ODA expenditures provided 36 000 new or ongoing jobs and led to contracts for 2 000 businesses, 50 universities and 60 colleges in Canada. These direct job benefits are proportionally greater than employment estimates attributed to Canadian exports because of the high labour intensity and Canadian content of goods and services utilised by CIDA."

[*Canadian International Development Agency* 1997-98 *Estimates*, Part III, *Expenditure Plan*, page 38]

CIDA's Part III Estimates also give specific examples of the benefits for Canada from its Geographic, Multilateral, Canadian Partnership and Countries in Transition programmes.

While in DAC terms the degree of aid tying in the Canadian programme is relatively high – in the sense that it is Canada, rather than its development country partners, that determines the procurement source – Canada itself considers that it provides significant flexibility in its procurement rules, for example, in terms of local procurement from other developing countries and balance-of-payments and budget support. CIDA's "untying" levels for bilateral assistance (other than food aid) are 50 per cent for least-developed countries and 33 per cent for all other developing countries. These limits are applied at the aggregate level, not for individual projects, which means that in practice goods and services can either be procured in Canada or the recipient country. In terms of DAC definitions, such aid is not classified untied as it is not open to procurement from other DAC countries. Canadian food aid, both multilateral and bilateral, is 90 per cent tied to Canadian sourcing. Canada's substantial multilateral assistance is essentially untied and IDRC activities are untied.

As regards the untying of aid, the Canadian partnerships philosophy leads strongly towards Canadian procurement. At the same time, the tying of aid impedes local ownership, involvement and responsibility in developing countries – which are now recognised, and certainly by Canada, as the most essential goals of development co-operation. Tied aid imposes extra costs on developing countries and is inconsistent with the OECD's advocacy of market approaches. While tied aid supports jobs in Canada, the tying of aid is not a cost-effective mechanism for subsidising employment, nor a panacea for export competitiveness. Other more direct forms of support would be more cost-effective. Many donors are currently reviewing their aid tying policies with a view to increasing untied aid. It would be timely for Canada to undertake an examination of the efficiency of tied aid as a means of supporting employment and exports in Canada and of the costs and benefits of tied aid for developing countries receiving Canadian ODA.

Part II

BASIC PROFILES

6

STRUCTURE OF CANADA'S DEVELOPMENT CO-OPERATION PROGRAMME

A. FUNDING

The International Assistance Envelope is the main source of funding for Canada's development co-operation programme. Some 95 per cent of activities funded by the Envelope qualify for recording as ODA, the remainder is official aid.

The Canadian International Development Agency manages the International Assistance Envelope and disburses nearly 80 per cent of Canada's ODA funded from the Envelope. The Department of Finance disburses approximately 11 per cent, the Department of Foreign Affairs and Trade allocates 5 per cent and the International Development Research Centre accounts for some 4 per cent. A diagram displaying the various federal departments and organisations involved in Canada's ODA programme is presented as Chart 1 in Chapter 2.

In addition to activities funded through the International Assistance Envelope, other costs and expenditures qualify for recording as ODA. These comprise, in descending order of magnitude in the 1997-98 fiscal year:

- costs of maintaining refugees during their first year in Canada (which Canada has included in its ODA since 1993-94);
- official bilateral debt relief for debt owed to institutions such as the Canadian Wheat Board and the Export Development Corporation;
- the imputed cost of tuition for students from developing countries;
- concessional financing through the Export Development Corporation;
- assistance by provincial governments;
- ODA-related administrative costs of some government departments and agencies; and
- imputed interest on advance payments.

These other ODA items totalled C$ 417 million in 1995-96 (16.1 per cent of total Canadian ODA in that fiscal year), C$ 594 million in 1996-97 (21.8 per cent) and were estimated at C$ 402 million in 1997-98 (16.7 per cent).

B. ORGANISATIONS

1. Canadian International Development Agency (CIDA)

Since the last DAC review of Canada in June 1994, CIDA has successively reported to four ministers: the Minister of Foreign Affairs, André Ouellet (November 1993 to January 1996) and three Ministers for International Co-operation – Pierre Pettigrew (January to October 1996), Don Boudria (October 1996 to June 1997) and Diane Marleau (from June 1997). The Minister for International Co-operation is also Minister responsible for the Francophonie and has a seat in Cabinet. Like other ministers with foreign policy portfolios, the Minister for International Co-operation is assisted by the Secretary of State for Asia-Pacific and the Secretary of State for Latin America and Africa.

The Canadian International Development Agency is headed by a President, an appointment at the Deputy Minister (Permanent Secretary) level. The President is supported by eight Vice-Presidents who, together with the Directors-General for Communications and Performance Review, manage CIDA's seven business lines: Geographic (divided between three Vice-Presidents); Multilateral; Canadian Partnership; Countries in Transition; Communications; Policy; and Human Resources and Corporate Services. CIDA's current organisational structure is presented in Chart 2.

The **Geographic programme** is CIDA's largest business line, absorbing 42.5 per cent of CIDA ODA funding for 1997-98. The programme's objective is to support sustainable development and poverty reduction by undertaking development programmes in keeping with the needs of developing countries,

Chart 2. Canadian International Development Agency (CIDA)

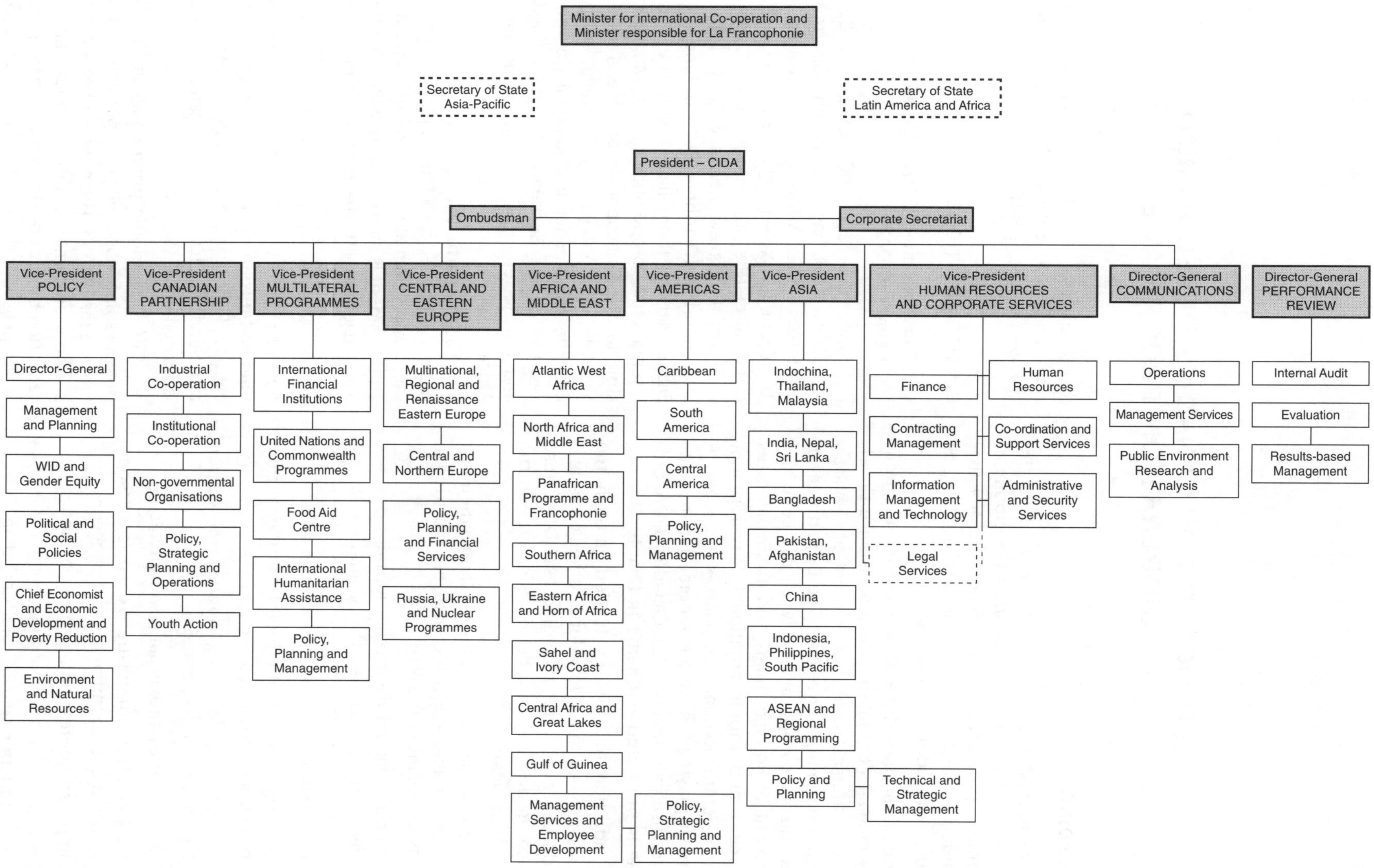

Secretary of State Asia-Pacific

Secretary of State Latin America and Africa

Minister for international Co-operation and Minister responsible for La Francophonie

Ombudsman

President – CIDA

Corporate Secretariat

Vice-President POLICY
- Director-General
- Management and Planning
- WID and Gender Equity
- Political and Social Policies
- Chief Economist and Economic Development and Poverty Reduction
- Environment and Natural Resources

Vice-President CANADIAN PARTNERSHIP
- Industrial Co-operation
- Institutional Co-operation
- Non-governmental Organisations
- Policy, Strategic Planning and Operations
- Youth Action

Vice-President MULTILATERAL PROGRAMMES
- International Financial Institutions
- United Nations and Commonwealth Programmes
- Food Aid Centre
- International Humanitarian Assistance
- Policy, Planning and Management

Vice-President CENTRAL AND EASTERN EUROPE
- Multinational, Regional and Renaissance Eastern Europe
- Central and Northern Europe
- Policy, Planning and Financial Services
- Russia, Ukraine and Nuclear Programmes

Vice-President AFRICA AND MIDDLE EAST
- Atlantic West Africa
- North Africa and Middle East
- Panafrican Programme and Francophonie
- Southern Africa
- Eastern Africa and Horn of Africa
- Sahel and Ivory Coast
- Central Africa and Great Lakes
- Gulf of Guinea
- Management Services and Employee Development
- Policy, Strategic Planning and Management

Vice-President AMERICAS
- Caribbean
- South America
- Central America
- Policy, Planning and Management

Vice-President ASIA
- Indochina, Thailand, Malaysia
- India, Nepal, Sri Lanka
- Bangladesh
- Pakistan, Afghanistan
- China
- Indonesia, Philippines, South Pacific
- ASEAN and Regional Programming
- Policy and Planning
- Technical and Strategic Management

Vice-President HUMAN RESOURCES AND CORPORATE SERVICES
- Human Resources
- Finance
- Co-ordination and Support Services
- Contracting Management
- Administrative and Security Services
- Information Management and Technology
- Legal Services

Director-General COMMUNICATIONS
- Operations
- Management Services
- Public Environment Research and Analysis

Director-General PERFORMANCE REVIEW
- Internal Audit
- Evaluation
- Results-based Management

Note: As of January 1998.
Source: CIDA.

the purpose and priorities of the ODA programme and Canada's foreign policy interests. The programme is divided between three branches – Africa and Middle East, which received 18.7 per cent of CIDA's funding; Asia, which received 15.4 per cent and Americas, 8.4 per cent. Almost 70 per cent of CIDA's Geographic programme focuses on low-income countries, with about three-quarters concentrated on 28 countries.

The second largest business line is the **Multilateral programme**, which received one-third of CIDA's 1997-98 funding. Its objectives are, first, to promote effective global and multilateral development approaches which reduce poverty, enhance human security and expand prosperity and, secondly, to ensure that Canadian humanitarian assistance and food aid to developing countries are appropriate, timely and effective. Canada contributes funds to the UN development programmes and humanitarian assistance organisations, the World Bank and the regional development banks – the African, Asian, Caribbean and Inter-American Development Banks – as part of CIDA's Multilateral programme. In consultation with DFAIT and the Department of Finance, CIDA is responsible for the daily monitoring and management of Canada's interests in these institutions, on behalf of the Minister of Foreign Affairs.

The objective of the **Canadian Partnership programme** is to promote mutually-beneficial partnerships between Canadian and developing-country organisations to support sustainable development and reduce poverty in the developing world. This programme, which covers NGOs, non-governmental institutions (such as universities, colleges, professional associations, unions and co-operatives) and private-sector partners, received 16.3 per cent of CIDA ODA funding in 1997-98.

The **Countries in Transition programme** (see Box 11) accounted for 5.8 per cent of 1997-98 funding.

The remaining three business lines were allocated small shares of CIDA's 1997-98 funding. The **Communications Branch's** objective is to improve public awareness of, and support for, the work of the Canadian co-operation programme and development partners (see Box 12). The **Policy Branch** aims to develop and recommend policies, expert advice and strategic plans in the area of sustainable development and to provide development information resources to CIDA. **Corporate Services** ensure that the Agency has the necessary support for the efficient and effective achievement of the international development assistance programme objectives within the framework of federal government policies, procedures and controls.

Box 11. **Assistance to Countries in Transition**

The Countries in Transition programme began in 1989, with projects in Hungary and Poland, and has developed quickly since then. Responsibility for the programme was transferred from DFAIT to CIDA in 1995. Today, the programme covers some 26 countries in all. In 1996, 13.5 per cent of Canada's assistance to Countries in Transition was eligible for recording as ODA, the remainder was official aid.

Reflecting the Canadian government's foreign policy priorities, as set out in *Canada in the World*, the programme mission is to support democratic development and economic liberalisation in Central and Eastern Europe by building mutually beneficial partnerships. Within the overall framework of promoting Canadian global interests and security, including nuclear safety, the programme objectives are:

- to assist the transition to market economies;
- to facilitate Canadian trade and investment links with the region; and
- to encourage good governance, democracy and adherence to international norms.

The programme is characterised by a large number of small, short-term actions and so is flexible and responsive to changing circumstances. CIDA has prepared country programme strategies, including specially tailored technical co-operation programmes, for 11 CEECs: the Czech Republic, Estonia, Hungary, Kazakstan, Latvia, Lithuania, Poland, Romania, Russia, the Slovak Republic and Ukraine. It is expected that, within the next five years, as the links between Canada and the Czech Republic, Hungary and Poland become increasingly characterised by conventional trade, economic and cultural relationships, CIDA's programme of technical co-operation with those countries will be wound down.

Box 12. **Public Opinion, Information and Development Education**

Canadian public support for aid has been described as "strong but soft". Opinion polling suggests that over 50 per cent of Canadians are strongly in favour of Canada's aid programme while a third are relatively neutral. Only ten per cent of Canadians oppose the programme. Support is stronger among young and better-educated Canadians.

Altruism and solidarity figure high among the principal factors driving Canadian opinion on aid. This translates into strong support for the provision of relief to victims of natural or human-induced disasters. Media attention on humanitarian crises contributes to the special interest in this aspect of the aid programme.

At the same time, a two-thirds majority place a higher priority on resolving Canada's fiscal problems than on improving the lives of the poor overseas. In the context of a difficult budgetary situation, with reductions in many domestic social programmes and concern over unemployment and Canada's national unity, issues relating to international development have elicited comparatively little public debate. The Canadian government's high-profile international initiatives in areas such as land mines and child labour have also tended to focus attention on a narrow set of issues, to the detriment of a wider debate on development challenges.

Other factors reducing support for development co-operation include a belief that aid does not reach its intended beneficiaries and an overestimation of the actual level of resources devoted by Canada to development co-operation.

CIDA's efforts in the area of public information include the dissemination of success stories, through the electronic and printed press. Examples include the "Heritage Minute", a one-minute television spot featuring the success of a Canadian-designed water pump, and the placement of inserts in such popular publications as *Homemakers, Madame au Foyer, Maclean's* and *L'Actualité*. CIDA makes use of new technologies such as Internet and CD-ROM to deliver its messages and works with partners to multiply opportunities. Senior CIDA officials also take part in direct outreach activities, focusing on local decision-makers and community and business partners.

2. Department of Finance

The Department of Finance is responsible for Canada's participation in the Bretton Woods institutions – the IMF and the World Bank – as well as the Paris Club and the European Bank for Reconstruction and Development. The Minister for Finance's annual report to Parliament on Canada's involvement in the Bretton Woods institutions is published as the *Report on Operations under the Bretton Woods and Related Agreements Act*.

3. Department of Foreign Affairs and International Trade (DFAIT)

Canada in the World describes the role of the Department of Foreign Affairs and International Trade as providing "leadership in helping to ensure the greatest possible coherence and synergy over the full range of the Government's international activities". The Department's top structure and the organisation of the Global and Security Policy Branch, which includes the Global and Human Issues Bureau created in 1995, and the Trade and Economic Policy Branch, are presented in Chart 3.

In addition to its policy co-ordination role, DFAIT undertakes development co-operation activities on its own account. DFAIT is responsible for certain grants and contributions to international organisations and the ODA-eligible costs related to Summits of the Francophonie. DFAIT manages the Canadian Commonwealth Scholarship and Fellowship Plan, which provides scholarships to students from Commonwealth countries, 46 of which are developing countries. While DFAIT is no longer involved in the delivery of Canada's assistance programme to CEECs, it retains broad policy responsibility in this area.

4. International Development Research Centre (IDRC)

The International Development Research Centre is a public corporation created by the Canadian Parliament in 1970 to initiate, encourage, support and conduct research into the problems of the developing regions of the world. It has an international Board of Governors and submits an annual report to Parliament through the Minister of Foreign Affairs. The Centre defines its mission as empowerment through knowledge and provides most of its

Chart 3. **Department of Foreign Affairs and International Trade (DFAIT)**

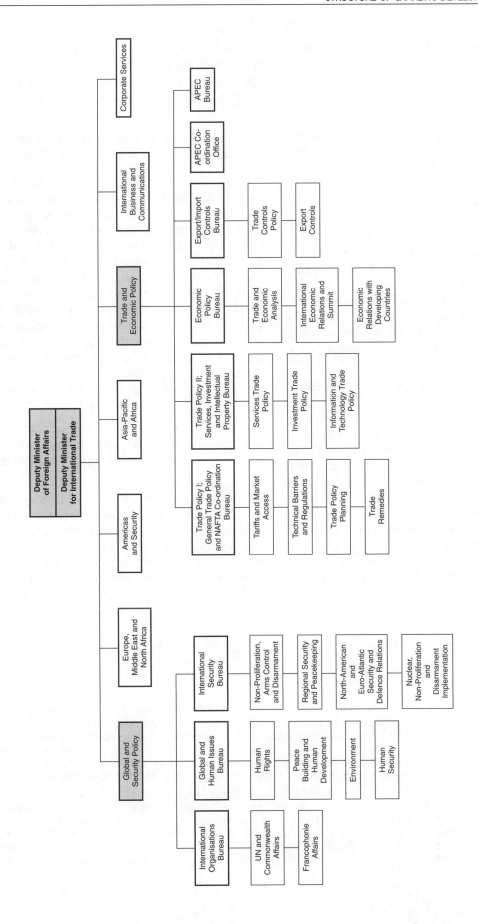

Source : DFAIT.

support to researchers and policy makers in developing countries.

The 1997-98 budget appropriation for IDRC was C$ 88.1 million, down from C$ 96.1 million in 1996-97. On 31 March 1996, IDRC had a total staff of 423 at its headquarters in Ottawa and regional offices in Cairo, Dakar, Johannesburg, Montevideo, Nairobi, New Delhi and Singapore – 103 of these were hired locally by the regional offices.

The IDRC's grant from the Canadian government has been reduced by more than 30 per cent over the last seven years. The Centre has consequently had to explore new ways of operating and obtaining finance (see Box 13). The IDRC has established a business development office to promote cofinancing arrangements with other donors and the private sector and has been successful in attracting around C$ 20 million in external funding annually – the equivalent of an increase in resources of more than one-fifth.

Since 1993, the IDRC's programme priorities have no longer been defined in sectoral terms, but in terms of six strategic development themes: food security; equity in natural resource use; biodiversity conservation; sustainable employment; strategies and policies for healthy societies; and information and communication, with work in this last area both complementing and supporting the five other themes. During 1997-2000, IDRC is pursuing these themes through 15 programme initiatives, each consisting of a network of research institutions focused on particular knowledge gaps, connected among themselves and with other relevant knowledge communities. This includes a programme on peacebuilding and reconstruction which supports

applied research in developing countries that can play a critical role in the development of analytical tools and can provide guidance on policy and action appropriate to a country's specific situation.

5. International Centre for Human Rights and Democratic Development (ICHRDD)

The International Centre for Human Rights and Democratic Development is a public corporation created by the Canadian Parliament in 1988. Its mandate is to defend and promote the rights and freedoms enshrined in the International Bill of Human Rights and to encourage the development of democratic societies. It has an international Board of Directors and submits an annual report to Parliament through the Minister of Foreign Affairs. The ICHRDD views itself as an activist organisation and seeks to fulfil its mandate by providing financial, political and technical support to front-line organisations and by speaking out about human rights abuses and advocating policies to reduce their incidence.

The Centre receives its funding through CIDA. For 1997-98, the Centre's appropriation is C$ 4.6 million as compared to C$ 5.0 million in previous fiscal years.

With a view to strengthening its impact and efficiency, the ICHRDD has undergone a period of strategic reflection. This led to the decision to reorient programmes away from 13 core countries in favour of a thematic approach, emphasizing four areas: women's rights as human rights; justice, rule of law and democratisation; trade investment and human rights; and indigenous rights.

Box 13. A New Approach to IDRC Programme Delivery

A sharp reduction in the IDRC's level of funding from the Canadian government has encouraged the Centre to explore alternative ways of undertaking its programmes. As a result, the delivery of many IDRC activities is now linked to a Secretariat, often housed within the Centre but overseen by an independent governing board who ensure that the appropriate research agenda is being pursued and that donor funds are being used efficiently. Ideally, these Secretariats will become self-sustaining and independent and "spin-off" from the IDRC. This has already occurred in several instances. In April 1997, the IDRC had 13 secretariats in operation.

An example of an IDRC cofinanced Secretariat is the Bellanet initiative. Bellanet focuses on the use of information technology to achieve greater donor efficiency and effectiveness, using Internet as the workspace for donor collaboration and project co-operation. The Bellanet Secretariat receives funding from CIDA; IDRC; the Dutch Directorate-General for International Co-operation; the MacArthur Foundation; the Rockefeller Foundation; the Swedish International Development Co-operation Agency; and the UN Development Programme. Further information on this initiative may be obtained from the Bellanet web site at http://www.bellanet.org.

6. Export Development Corporation

The Export Development Corporation is a crown corporation reporting to Parliament through the Minister for International Trade. It supplies a wide range of financial and risk management services including concessional export financing for commercial sales in developing countries that are not deemed to be creditworthy for other financing from the Corporation. For 1997-98, the Corporation has committed C$ 34 million for concessional export financing. On rare occasions and in collaboration with CIDA, the Corporation also offers associated financing. Both Canada's concessional export financing and associated financing meet the key Helsinki package tests.

7. Other departments and agencies

A number of other federal government departments and agencies administer small portions of Canada's development co-operation programme. The Department of Public Works and Government Services manages funding related to mandatory services such as acquisitions, transport management and major Crown projects. Funding in 1997-98 amounted to C$ 2.1 million. Heritage Canada is responsible for the extension of TV5 activities in Latin America and the Caribbean (1997-98 funding of C$ 0.2 million). Human Resources Development Canada, Environment Canada and the Departments of Justice, Agriculture and Health are also involved in the delivery of Canada's ODA programme.

BASIC PROFILES OF CANADIAN PROGRAMME

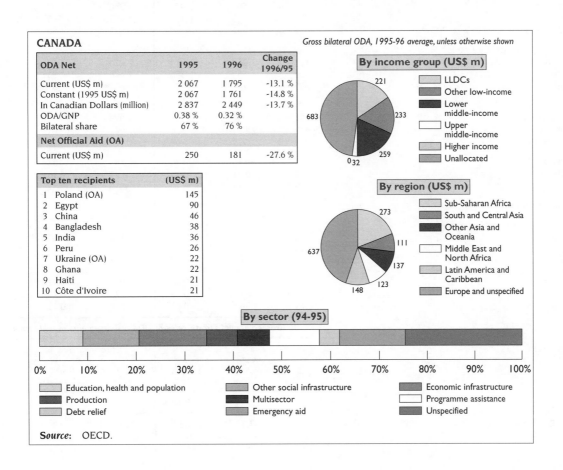

CANADA

Gross bilateral ODA, 1995-96 average, unless otherwise shown

ODA Net	1995	1996	Change 1996/95
Current (US$ m)	2 067	1 795	-13.1 %
Constant (1995 US$ m)	2 067	1 761	-14.8 %
In Canadian Dollars (million)	2 837	2 449	-13.7 %
ODA/GNP	0.38 %	0.32 %	
Bilateral share	67 %	76 %	
Net Official Aid (OA)			
Current (US$ m)	250	181	-27.6 %

Top ten recipients	(US$ m)
1 Poland (OA)	145
2 Egypt	90
3 China	46
4 Bangladesh	38
5 India	36
6 Peru	26
7 Ukraine (OA)	22
8 Ghana	22
9 Haiti	21
10 Côte d'Ivoire	21

By income group (US$ m)
- LLDCs
- Other low-income
- Lower middle-income
- Upper middle-income
- Higher income
- Unallocated

221, 233, 259, 032, 683

By region (US$ m)
- Sub-Saharan Africa
- South and Central Asia
- Other Asia and Oceania
- Middle East and North Africa
- Latin America and Caribbean
- Europe and unspecified

273, 111, 137, 123, 148, 637

By sector (94-95)

0% 10% 20% 30% 40% 50% 60% 70% 80% 90% 100%

- Education, health and population
- Other social infrastructure
- Economic infrastructure
- Production
- Multisector
- Programme assistance
- Debt relief
- Emergency aid
- Unspecified

Source: OECD.

A. ODA VOLUME AND OUTLOOK

Successive reductions in budget allocations for development assistance mean that although Canada still provides a significant ODA programme, it can no longer count itself among the most generous of DAC donors. Canada's ODA expressed as a share of gross national product was 0.32 per cent in 1996 (see Table 5), its lowest point in 30 years. Canada's ODA/GNP ratio remained above the DAC average (0.25 per cent) but was below the average country effort (unweighted average) of DAC Members (0.40 per cent). Its ratio was above the average for G7 countries (0.22 per cent) but half the average effort of the "like-minded" countries (0.64 per cent).

As reported in the last DAC Review, in 1993, Canada was the seventh most generous donor among the 21 DAC Member countries, but has now fallen to eleventh position in terms of the ODA/GNP ratio.

Canadian net disbursements of ODA fell to $1 795 million in 1996, a decline in real terms of 14.8 per cent from the 1995 level of $2 067 million. Official development assistance has fallen in real terms each year since 1993 (see Figure 1). In 1996, Canada was the ninth largest donor among DAC Member countries in terms of absolute aid volumes.

Table 5. **Main ODA volume indicators**

	i) Disbursements and commitments					
	Two-year averages over ten-year period			1994	1995	1996
	1985/86	1990/91	1995/96			
ODA net disbursements						
Current prices and exchange rates						
($ million)	1 663	2 537	1 931	2 250	2 067	1 795
Bilateral	1 026	1 740	1 371	1 423	1 385	1 356
Multilateral	637	797	560	827	682	439
1995 prices and exchange rates						
($ million)	2 154	2 268	1 914	2 276	2 067	1 761
Bilateral	1 328	1 555	1 358	1 440	1 385	1 330
Multilateral	825	713	556	837	682	431
National currency						
(C$ million)	2 291	2 933	2 643	3 073	2 837	2 449
Bilateral	1 413	2 011	1 876	1 943	1 901	1 850
Multilateral	878	922	767	1 129	936	599
GNP ratios (%)	0.49	0.45	0.35	0.43	0.38	0.32
Bilateral	0.30	0.31	0.25	0.27	0.25	0.24
Multilateral	0.19	0.14	0.10	0.16	0.12	0.08
ODA commitments						
Current prices and exchange rates						
($ million)	1 770	2 655	2 224	2 110	2 240	2 207
Bilateral	1 175	1 787	1 583	1 356	1 620	1 547
Multilateral	595	868	640	754	620	661
GNP ratios (%)	0.52	0.47	0.40	0.40	0.41	0.39
Bilateral	0.34	0.32	0.28	0.26	0.30	0.27
Multilateral	0.17	0.15	0.11	0.14	0.11	0.12

	ii) Average annual growth rates of ODA disbursements in real terms					
				For reference: Total DAC		
	1985/86-1990/91	1990/91-1995/96	1985/86-1995/96	1985/86-1990/91	1990/91-1995/96	1985/86-1995/96
	Percentages					
Total ODA	1.0	−3.3	−1.2	3.1	−3.2	−0.1
Bilateral	3.2	−2.7	0.2	3.7	−4.0	−0.2
Multilateral	−2.9	−4.8	−3.9	1.7	−1.2	0.2
For reference:						
GNP growth in real terms	2.7	1.7	2.2	3.4	2.4	2.9

	iii) Share in total DAC					
	Two-year averages over ten-year period			1994	1995	1996
	1985/86	1990/91	1995/96			
	Percentages					
Total ODA	5.2	4.6	3.4	3.8	3.5	3.2
Bilateral	4.4	4.3	3.4	3.4	3.4	3.5
Multilateral	7.2	5.1	3.2	4.6	3.7	2.7
Gross national product	3.6	3.4	2.5	2.6	2.5	2.6

Source : OECD.

The decrease in ODA volume in 1996 can be partially explained by fact that Canada's annual contribution to IDA fell outside the 1996 calendar year – the contribution for the 1995-96 fiscal year (1 April to 31 March) was made on 30 November 1995, while the 1996-97 contribution occurred on 12 March 1997. Had this second contribution taken place in 1996, Canada's ODA would have been some $159 million larger, *i.e.* approximately $1 954 million. Should the 1997-98 IDA contribution also occur during the 1997 calendar year, Canada's 1997 ODA volume will be buoyed up by having two IDA contributions in the same year and the projected further decline in ODA will appear less severe than expected.

B. COMPOSITION AND SECTORAL DISTRIBUTION OF AID

A feature of the Canadian programme is its strong support to multilateral institutions. Canada has traditionally devoted a higher share of its ODA to multilateral contributions than the DAC average (see Table 6), although in 1996 this was not the case, partially because of the timing of IDA contributions. Canada was a strong supporter of the World Food Programme (two-year average of 6.6 per cent of total net ODA in 1990/91) and the regional development banks (4.9 per cent in 1990/91), but the share of Canadian ODA directed to these institutions has fallen in recent years (World Food Programme:

3.8 per cent in 1996 and regional development banks: 2.0 per cent in 1996). Multilateral contributions have been disproportionately affected by the decline in Canadian ODA, falling at an annual average rate of 4.8 per cent in real terms between 1990/91 and 1995/96.

As regards bilateral ODA, the largest components are project and programme aid (20.8 per cent of total net ODA in 1996) and technical co-operation (18.4 per cent). Bilateral food aid is decreasing, but at 4.6 per cent in 1996 is still about twice the DAC average. Emergency aid has become a large share since 1993, following Canada's decision to include as part of its ODA the costs of maintaining refugees (such as food, shelter and training costs) during their first year in the country (see Table 7). At 10.1 per cent of total net ODA in 1996, support to NGOs is another large share of the Canadian programme, as compared to the DAC average of around 2.0 per cent. No associated financing has been offered since 1992.

Table 8 shows the sectoral distribution of Canada's ODA. The trend over the last decade has been a shift from production sectors – agriculture, forestry, fishing and mining – to social infrastructure and services, especially actions to develop government and civil society, and multisector projects. Declines in commodity aid and general programme assistance have been off set by increases in the

Table 6. **Share of total ODA net disbursements to multilateral agencies**

Percentages

	1993	1994	1995	1996
Canada	32.4	36.8	33.0	24.5
Total DAC (including contributions to EC)	30.3	30.2	31.1	29.5
Total DAC (excluding contributions to EC)	23.1	22.2	22.0	21.7

Table 7. **The effect of the inclusion of refugee costs on Canada's ODA**

	1992	1993	1994	1995	1996
Costs reported of maintaining refugees during their first year in Canada ($ million)	0	183.7	153.2	111.5	120.0
ODA/GNP ratio (percentages)					
Including costs of maintaining refugees	0.46	0.45	0.43	0.38	0.32
Excluding costs of maintaining refugees	0.46	0.42	0.40	0.36	0.30

Table 8. **Distribution of bilateral ODA commitments by major purposes**

	1985/86		1990/91		1995/96		For reference: Total DAC 1994/95 % of total
	$ million	% of total	$ million	% of total	$ million	% of total	
Social infrastructure and services	**182**	**15.5**	**292**	**16.3**	**384**	**24.2**	**28.9**
Education	95	8.1	164	9.1	128	8.1	11.0
Health	28	2.4	35	2.0	43	2.7	3.8
Population programmes	–	–	2	0.1	30	1.9	1.4
Water supply and sanitation	28	2.4	34	1.9	27	1.7	5.4
Government and civil society	12	1.0	19	1.1	97	6.1	2.9
Other social infrastructure and services	19	1.6	38	2.1	60	3.8	4.3
Economic infrastructure and services	**169**	**14.4**	**224**	**12.5**	**184**	**11.6**	**22.6**
Transport and storage	92	7.9	56	3.1	71	4.5	9.8
Communications	20	1.7	63	3.5	20	1.3	1.6
Energy	51	4.3	51	2.9	51	3.2	9.0
Banking and financial services	6	0.5	1	0.0	31	2.0	0.6
Business and other services	–	–	54	3.0	11	0.7	1.6
Production sectors	**312**	**26.6**	**256**	**14.3**	**106**	**6.7**	**10.6**
Agriculture, forestry and fishing	221	18.8	152	8.5	64	4.0	7.4
Industry, mining and construction	91	7.8	101	5.6	42	2.7	1.7
– Industry	6	0.5	57	3.2	36	2.2	1.1
– Mining	85	7.2	2	0.1	6	0.4	0.2
– Construction	0	0.0	8	0.4	0	0.0	0.1
Trade and tourism	1	0.1	3	0.1	1	0.0	1.2
– Trade	0	0.0	1	0.1	0	0.0	0.6
– Tourism	0	0.0	1	0.1	0	0.0	0.1
Other	–	–	0	0.0	0	0.0	0.2
Multisector	**33**	**2.8**	**68**	**3.8**	**142**	**9.0**	**4.5**
Total sector allocable	**696**	**59.2**	**839**	**46.9**	**816**	**51.6**	**66.6**
Commodity aid and general programme assistance	226	19.2	280	15.7	140	8.8	6.7
Action relating to debt	2	0.1	2	0.1	127	8.0	9.5
Emergency assistance	41	3.5	65	3.7	170	10.7	5.2
Administrative costs of donors	77	6.6	171	9.6	117	7.4	4.7
Support to NGOs	117	10.0	261	14.6	190	12.0	1.0
Unallocated	17	1.4	168	9.4	24	1.5	6.4
Total	**1 175**	**100.0**	**1 787**	**100.0**	**1 583**	**100.0**	**100.0**

share of ODA for debt forgiveness and emergency assistance.

C. FINANCIAL TERMS AND DEBT FORGIVENESS

In response to the growing debt problem of developing countries, Canada now has an all-grants programme. Most ODA loans have been rescheduled or forgiven. Canada encourages the immediate forgiveness of all remaining ODA debt owed by heavily-indebted poor countries to Paris Club creditors and urges other donors to provide future ODA to HIPC countries in grant or near-grant form.

Among developing countries, Egypt has been the main beneficiary of Canadian debt forgiveness actions since the last DAC Review. In 1993, Canada forgave $43 million of debt owed by Egypt, followed by a further $56 million in 1995 and $96 million in 1996. Together, these actions account for over 80 per cent of net Canadian ODA to Egypt since 1993 and represent nearly half the developing country debt forgiven by Canada during the same period. Several Latin American and Caribbean countries have received debt forgiveness in recent years, most notably Jamaica ($72 million in 1993), Guyana ($29 million in 1993) and Barbados ($18 million in 1993). Seven Latin American countries have also benefited from debt reduction to a total value of $110 million (as at the end of 1996) as a result of the 1992 Latin American Debt Conversion Initiative. In sub-Saharan Africa, Tanzania had $17 million of debt forgiven in 1995, Côte d'Ivoire had $14 million forgiven in 1995 and an additional $12 million in 1996,

Table 9. **Geographically unallocated ODA**

	1995	1996
Canadian NGOs	174.8	153.4
Food aid through Canadian NGOs	82.6	10.8
International NGOs	19.5	28.0
Scholarships	13.1	14.3
Imputed student costs	50.0	47.7
Imputed interest on advance payments	3.3	3.3
Costs of maintaining refugees during their first year in Canada	111.5	120.0
Public awareness	3.3	1.9
Administrative costs	114.0	115.9
Miscellaneous	57.0	47.5
TOTAL GEOGRAPHICALLY UNALLOCATED	**629.0**	**542.8**

Source : CIDA.

while $13 million of debt owed by Zambia was forgiven in 1995.

D. GEOGRAPHICAL DISTRIBUTION

Canada in the World commits Canada to continuing to provide most of its ODA to low-income countries, to devote the highest share of resources to Africa and to focus efforts on a limited number of countries. These commitments replace the former planning framework for Canadian ODA, specified in the 1988 strategy *Sharing our Future*, which included the objectives of directing 65 per cent of bilateral assistance to Commonwealth and Francophone developing countries, providing 75 per cent of bilateral aid to low-income and small island states and concentrating 75 per cent of bilateral aid on 30 countries or regional groupings.

A large share of Canada's ODA is reported to the Secretariat as "unspecified" (in 1995/96, one third of total gross ODA disbursements was bilateral aid not allocated to a particular recipient country or region). The uses of Canada's geographically unallocated ODA are shown in Table 9. Canada would be able to report the first three items in the table by country, but present reporting arrangements do not allow for this.

In 1995/96, half of Canada's net disbursements of bilateral ODA were reported allocated to particular recipients. Of this, 61.6 per cent was directed to low-income countries and 51.4 per cent benefited countries in Africa. Egypt, China, Bangladesh, Ghana and Haiti were the principal beneficiaries of Canadian ODA in 1995/96 and received collectively 31.4 per cent of allocable bilateral assistance (see Table 10). The 20 largest beneficiaries in those years (13 of which were low-income countries and 10 African) received two-thirds of Canada's bilateral aid, the same share as in 1990/91 but lower than the share in 1985/86. In 1995/96, a total of 124 countries received development assistance from Canada.

E. OFFICIAL AID

Net disbursements of Canadian official aid to countries and territories on Part II of the DAC List of aid recipients[9] amounted to $181 million in 1996, corresponding to 0.03 per cent of GNP. Canada's OA has fluctuated over recent years, due to some large debt forgiveness actions. Canada has forgiven a significant part of the interest due on export credits extended to Poland by the Export Development Corporation and the Canadian Wheat Board: $180 million in 1992, $152 million in 1995 and $127 million in 1996. These actions make Poland the largest beneficiary of Canadian OA. Other major recipients of OA have been Russia ($13 million in 1996) and Ukraine ($14 million in 1996). Canadian OA also includes annual disbursements of around $25 million to the European Bank for Reconstruction and Development, although no contribution fell during the 1996 calendar year.

F. AID REPORTING

Canada is a model contributor to the Creditor Reporting System, in terms of the quality, accuracy and timeliness of processing transactions. On numerous occasions, the close collaboration that has developed between CIDA and the OECD Secretariat has resulted in improvements to statistical systems, as well as clarification and simplification of procedures. To fulfil its reporting obligations, Canada allocates about two person years for reporting on its development co-operation programme.

Table 10. **Major recipients of bilateral ODA net disbursements**

Rank	1985/86				1990/91				1995/96			
	Recipient	Constant 1995 $ million	% of bilateral allocable	Cumulative % of bilateral allocable	Recipient	Constant 1995 $ million	% of bilateral allocable	Cumulative % of bilateral allocable	Recipient	Constant 1995 $ million	% of bilateral allocable	Cumulative % of bilateral allocable
1	Bangladesh	97	10.5	10.5	Bangladesh	88	9.9	9.9	Egypt	88	12.9	12.9
2	Pakistan	67	7.2	17.7	China	48	5.5	15.4	China	46	6.7	19.6
3	India	57	6.2	24.0	Indonesia	41	4.6	20.0	Bangladesh	37	5.5	25.1
4	Indonesia	56	6.0	30.0	Ghana	30	3.4	23.4	Ghana	22	3.2	28.2
5	Tanzania	37	4.0	34.0	Egypt	30	3.4	26.9	Haiti	21	3.1	31.4
6	Ethiopia	35	3.8	37.8	Pakistan	30	3.4	30.3	Côte d'Ivoire	21	3.1	34.5
7	Kenya	31	3.4	41.2	Mozambique	29	3.2	33.5	India	21	3.1	37.5
8	Sri Lanka	28	3.1	44.3	Tanzania	29	3.2	36.7	Rwanda	18	2.7	40.2
9	Jamaica	26	2.9	47.1	Cameroon	28	3.1	39.9	States ex-Yugoslavia	18	2.7	42.9
10	Sudan	25	2.7	49.8	Ethiopia	27	3.0	42.9	Philippines	18	2.6	45.5
11	Ghana	22	2.4	52.2	Jamaica	25	2.8	45.7	Peru	18	2.6	48.1
12	China	22	2.3	54.6	Thailand	24	2.7	48.4	Tanzania	17	2.5	50.6
13	Niger	22	2.3	56.9	Philippines	23	2.6	51.0	Indonesia	17	2.5	53.1
14	Senegal	21	2.2	59.1	Senegal	22	2.5	53.5	Mali	15	2.2	55.3
15	Thailand	20	2.2	61.3	Morocco	22	2.5	56.0	Cameroon	15	2.2	57.5
16	Peru	20	2.1	63.5	India	21	2.4	58.4	Senegal	15	2.2	59.7
17	Zaire	19	2.1	65.6	Zimbabwe	20	2.2	60.6	Zambia	14	2.1	61.8
18	Mali	18	2.0	67.6	Jordan	19	2.2	62.8	Thailand	13	1.8	63.6
19	Zimbabwe	18	2.0	69.6	Mali	18	2.1	64.9	Bolivia	12	1.7	65.3
20	Cameroon	18	2.0	71.6	Zambia	17	1.9	66.8	Zimbabwe	11	1.6	66.9
	Total bilateral allocable	**922**	**100.0**	**100.0**	**Total bilateral allocable**	**886**	**100.0**	**100.0**	**Total bilateral allocable**	**681**	**100.0**	**100.0**
	Unallocated (additional to total shown)	405	43.9		Unallocated (additional to total shown)	661	74.5		Unallocated (additional to total shown)	677	99.5	
	Memo item: Total number of recipients	122			*Memo item:* Total number of recipients	122			*Memo item:* Total number of recipients	124		

Source: OECD.

NOTES

1. The North-South Institute is an independent, non-profit corporation providing research on relations between industrialised and developing countries.

2. The Conference Board of Canada is an independent applied research organisation providing information and analysis on economic, management and public policy issues.

3. Assuming constant GNP growth at current rates: around 3.5 per cent each year in real terms or approximately 5 per cent in nominal terms.

4. See *OECD Economic Surveys*, Canada 1996-97, page 4.

5. IDRC was given special responsibilities at the Rio de Janeiro conference for assisting developing countries in follow-up to Agenda 21. This led to significant changes in the Centre's programming and reinforced its global role in promoting sustainable and equitable development through research.

6. "Military goods" are defined as goods specifically designed or adapted for military use and controlled under Group 2 (Munitions) of Canada's *Export Control List*.

7. See *Canadian Development Report 1996-97*, The North-South Institute, page 4.

8. DAC Members have agreed that administrative costs and technical co-operation expenditure should be disregarded in assessing the share of ODA which is tied, partially tied or untied.

9. Part II of the DAC list of aid recipients comprises the more advanced Central and Eastern European Countries and New Independent States of the former Soviet Union (CEECs/NIS), and the more advanced developing countries and territories.

PRESS RELEASE OF THE DAC AID REVIEW OF CANADA

The Canadian Government's foreign policy statement, *Canada in the World*, reaffirmed Canada's commitment to play an active role in international efforts towards global peace and prosperity and set out a range of ambitious goals for its development co-operation programme. Canada's co-sponsorship of the Global Knowledge Conference in Toronto in June 1997 was evidence of the energy and innovativeness of this commitment applied to the challenges of development co-operation. Canada is also playing an active role on other parts of the evolving international agenda for development partnerships.

The reach and depth of Canada's international involvement – clearly rooted in the country's values, interests and capabilities – have not been matched by commensurate levels of resources allocated for development co-operation in recent years. To respond to the domestic public debt burden, the government instituted public sector expenditure cuts, including international assistance programmes. Canada's official development assistance (ODA) has declined significantly, from an average of approximately 0.45 per cent of gross national product (GNP) at the beginning of the 1990s to 0.32 per cent in 1996, its lowest point in 30 years, and it is projected to fall still further by 1998-99, to below 0.30 per cent.

The government's intentions with regard to future funding levels for Canada's international assistance will be announced in early 1998 when the Minister of Finance tables the federal budget in Parliament. As the government has restored stability to its fiscal situation, this will be a critical moment for the future of Canada's ODA programme, and for Canada's valued international role.

James Michel, Chair of the Development Assistance Committee (DAC), who presided at the DAC's regular triennial peer review of the development co-operation of Canada, summarised the DAC Peer Review of Canada:

- The Committee noted that the priorities set in 1995 for Canada's development assistance programme – basic human needs; gender equity; infrastructure services; human rights, democracy, good governance; private sector development; and the environment – are matched closely by the common strategy document *Shaping the 21st Century: The Contribution of Development Co-operation*, adopted by DAC Members in May 1996 in the development of which Canada played an active role.

- The Committee appreciated Canada's emphasis on formulating coherent responses to current and future global challenges, and the high degree of inter-departmental co-ordination taking place in policy formulation in the area of trade and other important policy areas affecting development. Institutions such as the International Development Research Centre (IDRC), the International Centre for Human Rights and Democratic Development (ICHRDD) and the International Institute for Sustainable Development (IISD) provide a range of special development contributions over and beyond the purely governmental mechanisms.

- The Committee appreciated the steps being made by the Canadian International Development Agency (CIDA) to build the human rights and governance dimension into its programme priorities and, with the Department of Foreign Affairs and International Trade, to create a new structure for rapid responses to conflict and emergency situations in developing countries, drawing in the expertise of NGOs. Major foreign policy initiatives (as in the piloting of the new treaty banning anti-personnel landmines) are also making notable contributions.

- The reductions in ODA raise concerns about Canada's ability to meet expectations, both at home and internationally. A growing range of goals, together with Canada's involvement in a large array of issues and with a wide range of partners and multilateral organisations, also brings into sharper focus the issue of the dispersion of Canadian efforts, a concern the Committee had already raised in previous reviews.

- The Committee commended the comprehensive and thorough renewal process being undertaken by the CIDA to equip the Agency with the necessary human resources and institutional structures to tackle its ambitious mission. CIDA is among the pioneers in the DAC in redirecting its programmes from a traditional sector-focus to a theme-based approach, with a concentration on actual results rather than inputs. These promising efforts will deserve careful monitoring (and upgrading of information systems) and should yield valuable lessons for other donors facing similar challenges.

- Like many DAC donor agencies, CIDA must reconcile the needs and primary responsibilities of developing country partners with the demanding accountability criteria required by the Government and public of Canada. Efforts are being launched in the DAC to explore how to resolve these issues.

- CIDA also has to respond to the multiple objectives and interests of CIDA's Canadian partners, both in the voluntary and private sectors. Canada's extensive use of tied aid illustrates this tension. As part of the Canadian government's overall concern with accountability and the impact of public expenditures, there would seem to be a strong case for Canada, like other donors, to re-examine the efficiency of tied aid in relation to other means of promoting competitive exports and employment at home.

- The Committee also raised questions regarding the re-centralisation of aid management by Canada following a major decentralisation initiative some years earlier. A number of other DAC Members are finding that the demands of improved field-based partnerships and donor co-ordination in developing countries, notably in complex areas such as poverty reduction and governance, call for a strengthened field presence.

- Canada has significantly improved the orientation of its food aid which is now targeted towards reducing poverty and malnutrition, notably among women and children.

Mr John M. Robinson, Vice President, Policy, Canadian International Development Agency, led the Delegation of Canada to the review session. The Netherlands and New Zealand were the examining countries.

Canada: Comparative aid performance

	ODA net disbursements 1996 $ million	ODA net disbursements 1996 % of GDP	Average annual growth in real term (%) 1985/86-1995/96	Grant element of ODA commitments (%) 1996[a]	Aid appropriations as a share of central government budget (%) 1996	Share of multilateral aid 1996 % of ODA excl. EC	Share of multilateral aid 1996 % of ODA incl. EC	Share of multilateral aid 1996 % of GNP excl. EC	Share of multilateral aid 1996 % of GNP incl. EC	ODA to LLDCs Bilateral and imputed multilateral 1996 % of ODA	ODA to LLDCs Bilateral and imputed multilateral 1996 % of GNP
Australia	1 074	0.28	-0.6	100.0	1.2	20.7		0.06		20.4	0.06
Austria	557	0.24	2.1	97.5	..	9.1	26.0	0.02	0.06	13.8	0.03
Belgium	913	0.34	-1.4	99.1	..	21.5	42.0	0.07	0.14	24.1	0.08
Canada	**1 795**	**0.32**	**-1.2**	**100.0**	**1.4**	**24.5**		**0.08**		**19.0**	**0.06**
Denmark	1 772	1.04	3.7	94.1	2.7	35.6	40.3	0.37	0.42	31.5	0.33
Finland	408	0.34	-1.5	97.3	1.0	35.6	47.4	0.12	0.16	28.8	0.10
France	7 451	0.48	0.8	92.3	..	11.4	22.8	0.06	0.11	19.0	0.09
Germany	7 601	0.33	0.1	91.7	..	22.5	40.3	0.07	0.13	22.3	0.07
Ireland	179	0.31	7.0	100.0	..	13.4	36.2	0.04	0.11	42.4	0.13
Italy	2 416	0.20	-4.3	99.5	..	43.6	66.4	0.09	0.13	24.5	0.05
Japan	9 439	0.20	1.6	78.2	..	13.1		0.03		15.0	0.03
Luxembourg	82	0.44	11.3	100.0		14.1	31.2	0.06	0.14	26.8	0.12
Netherlands	3 246	0.81	1.2	100.0	3.6	22.4	29.9	0.18	0.24	27.7	0.23
New Zealand	122	0.21	-0.5	100.0	0.6	16.2		0.03		21.2	0.04
Norway	1 311	0.85	1.0	99.3	1.8	28.0		0.24		38.7	0.33
Portugal	218	0.21	18.7	100.0	..	3.5	27.9	0.01	0.06	67.8	0.14
Spain	1 251	0.22	12.3	89.6	1.0	7.6	29.1	0.02	0.06	11.3	0.02
Sweden	1 999	0.84	0.5	100.0	..	24.9	30.2	0.21	0.25	28.7	0.24
Switzerland	1 026	0.34	2.4	100.0	2.8	29.6		0.10		29.6	0.10
United Kingdom	3 199	0.27	1.0	96.4	1.1	21.9	44.0	0.06	0.12	25.3	0.07
United States	9 377	0.12	-4.1	99.6	..	26.2		0.03		13.4	0.02
Total DAC	55 438	0.25	-0.1	91.8		21.2	29.5	0.05	0.07	20.6	0.05

Memo: Average country effort   0.40

Notes:
.. Indicates that data are not available.
a) Excluding debt reorganisation.

Net ODA from DAC countries in 1996

As % of GNP

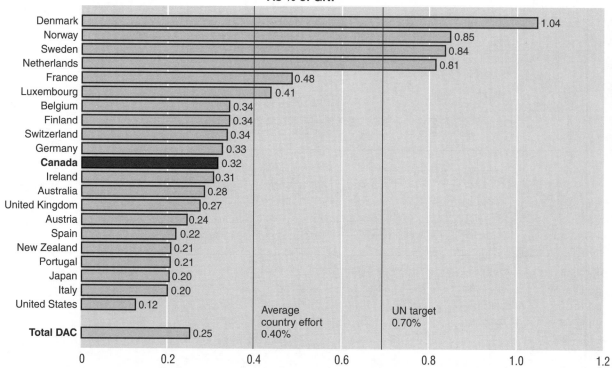

Denmark	1.04
Norway	0.85
Sweden	0.84
Netherlands	0.81
France	0.48
Luxembourg	0.41
Belgium	0.34
Finland	0.34
Switzerland	0.34
Germany	0.33
Canada	0.32
Ireland	0.31
Australia	0.28
United Kingdom	0.27
Austria	0.24
Spain	0.22
New Zealand	0.21
Portugal	0.21
Japan	0.20
Italy	0.20
United States	0.12
Total DAC	0.25

Average country effort 0.40%

UN target 0.70%

$ billion

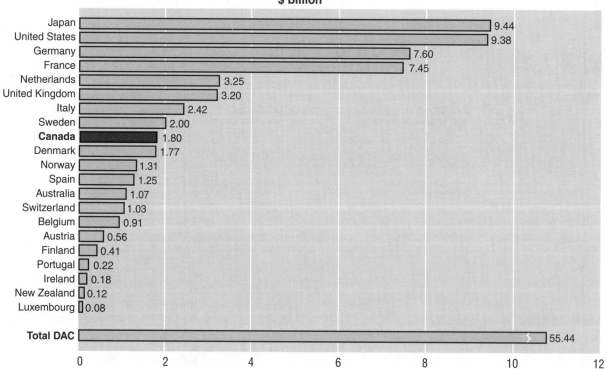

Japan	9.44
United States	9.38
Germany	7.60
France	7.45
Netherlands	3.25
United Kingdom	3.20
Italy	2.42
Sweden	2.00
Canada	1.80
Denmark	1.77
Norway	1.31
Spain	1.25
Australia	1.07
Switzerland	1.03
Belgium	0.91
Austria	0.56
Finland	0.41
Portugal	0.22
Ireland	0.18
New Zealand	0.12
Luxembourg	0.08
Total DAC	55.44

Source: OECD.

DESCRIPTION OF KEY TERMS

The following brief descriptions of the main development co-operation terms used in this publication are provided for general background information. Full definitions of these and other related terms can be found in the "Glossary of Key Terms and Concepts" published in the DAC's annual Development Co-operation Report.

ASSOCIATED FINANCING: The combination of OFFICIAL DEVELOPMENT ASSISTANCE, whether GRANTS or LOANS, with any other funding to form finance packages.

DAC (DEVELOPMENT ASSISTANCE COMMITTEE): The committee of the OECD which deals with development co-operation matters. A description of its aims and a list of its Members are given at the front of this volume.

DAC LIST OF AID RECIPIENTS: A two-part List of Aid Recipients was introduced by the DAC with effect from 1 January 1994. Part I of the List is presented in the following categories (the word "countries" includes territories):

LLDCs: Least Developed Countries. Group established by the United Nations. To be classified as an LLDC, countries must fall below thresholds established for income, economic diversification and social development.

Other LICs: Other Low-Income Countries. Includes all non-LLDC countries with per capita GNP less than $765 in 1995 (World Bank Atlas basis).

LMICs: Lower Middle-Income Countries, *i.e.* with GNP per capita (World Bank Atlas basis) between $766 and $3 035 in 1995.

UMICs: Upper Middle-Income Countries, *i.e.* with GNP per capita (World Bank Atlas basis) between $3 036 and $9 385 in 1995.

HICs: High-Income Countries, *i.e.* with GNP per capita (World Bank Atlas basis) more than $9 385 in 1995.

Part II of the List comprises "Countries in Transition". These comprise: *i*) more advanced Central and Eastern European Countries and the New Indepen-

dent States of the former Soviet Union; and *ii*) more advanced developing countries.

DEBT REORGANISATION: Any action officially agreed between creditor and debtor that alters the terms previously established for repayment. This may include forgiveness, rescheduling or refinancing.

DISBURSEMENT: The release of funds to, or the purchase of goods or services for a recipient; by extension, the amount thus spent. They may be recorded **gross** (the total amount disbursed over a given accounting period) or **net** (less any repayments of LOAN principal during the same period).

EXPORT CREDITS: LOANS for the purpose of trade and which are not represented by a negotiable financial instrument. Frequently these LOANS bear interest at a rate subsidised by the government of the creditor country as a means of promoting exports.

GRANTS: Transfers made in cash, goods or services for which no repayment is required.

GRANT ELEMENT: Reflects the **financial terms** of a transaction: interest rate, maturity and grace period (*i.e.* the interval to the first repayment of principal). The grant element is nil for a LOAN carrying an interest rate of 10 per cent; it is 100 per cent for a GRANT; and it lies between these two limits for a soft LOAN.

LOANS: Transfers for which repayment is required. Data on **net loans** include deductions for repayments of principal (but not payment of interest) on earlier loans.

OFFICIAL AID: Flows which meet the conditions of eligibility for inclusion in OFFICIAL DEVELOPMENT ASSISTANCE, except that the recipients are on Part II of the DAC LIST OF AID RECIPIENTS.

OFFICIAL DEVELOPMENT ASSISTANCE (ODA): GRANTS or LOANS to countries and territories on Part I of the DAC LIST OF AID RECIPIENTS (developing countries) provided by the official sector with the promotion of economic development and welfare as the main objective and which are at concessional financial terms (if a LOAN, having a GRANT ELEMENT of at least 25 per cent).

OTHER OFFICIAL FLOWS (OOF): Transactions by the official sector with countries on the DAC LIST OF AID RECIPIENTS which do not meet the conditions for eligibility as OFFICIAL DEVELOPMENT ASSISTANCE or OFFICIAL AID.

PARTIALLY UNTIED AID: OFFICIAL DEVELOPMENT ASSISTANCE (or OFFICIAL AID) for which the associated goods and services must be procured in the donor country or among a restricted group of other countries, which must however include substantially all aid recipient countries.

PRIVATE NON-CONCESSIONAL FLOWS: Consist of the following flows at market terms financed out of private sector resources:

Direct investment: Investment made to acquire or add to a lasting interest in an enterprise in a country on the DAC LIST OF AID RECIPIENTS.

Bilateral portfolio investment: Includes bank lending, and the purchase of shares, bonds and real estate.

Multilateral portfolio investment: This covers the transactions of the private non-bank and bank sector in the securities issued by multilateral institutions.

Private export credits: See EXPORT CREDITS.

TECHNICAL CO-OPERATION: Includes both i) GRANTS to nationals of aid recipient countries receiving education or training at home or abroad, and ii) payments to consultants, advisers and similar personnel as well as teachers and administrators serving in recipient countries.

TIED AID: Official GRANTS or LOANS where procurement of the goods or services involved is limited to the donor country or to a group of countries which does not include substantially all aid recipients.

UNTIED AID: OFFICIAL DEVELOPMENT ASSISTANCE (or OFFICIAL AID) for which the associated goods and services may be fully and freely procured in substantially all countries.

VOLUME: Unless otherwise stated, data are expressed in current United States dollars. Data in national currencies are converted into dollars using annual average exchange rates. To give a truer idea of the volume of flows over time, some data are presented in **constant prices and exchange rates**, with a reference year specified. This means that adjustment has been made to cover both inflation between the year in question and the reference year, and changes in the exchange rate between the currency concerned and the United States dollar over the same period.

OECD PUBLICATIONS, 2, rue André-Pascal, 75775 PARIS CEDEX 16
PRINTED IN FRANCE
(43 98 10 1 P) ISBN 92-64-16098-1 – No. 50243 1998